entertainment purposes only. All effort has been executed to present accurate, up to date, reliable, complete information. No warranties of any kind are declared or implied. Readers acknowledge that the author is not engaging in the rendering of legal, financial, medical or professional advice. The content within this book has been derived from various sources. Please consult a licensed professional before attempting any techniques outlined in this book.

By reading this document, the reader agrees that under no circumstances is the author responsible for any losses, direct or indirect, that are incurred as a result of the use of information contained within this document, including, but not limited to, errors, omissions, or inaccuracies.

Introduction

What is one of the most important skills to have in this century? If you guessed programming, you are right on the money. With the internet's growth, coding has become instrumental in creating environments on the internet and through applications. The problem, however, is the lack of coding experience needed with many jobs. Even if someone opens a flower shop, it is essential to have a computer-based program that will input data and adapt to changes within the business. Thousands, if not millions, of business owners are looking for people who have experience in coding, and the highest demand is for people who are more than a little comfortable with the processes. If you are looking for a new career in programming, you have come to the right place.

This book is designed with understanding code in mind. What does that mean? It means that this book will give you the basics of programming to get you started on your journey. You might be saying, "Well, where do the basics give me?" A foundation in the basics of programming is a skill that most people do not have, and practicing with your newly-found passion for programming will springboard you into more advanced applications and literature.

The information in this book has been gathered from Python websites (such as Pycharm, python programming, pyladies, and the Python website itself), universities, and other online educational websites. This book contains real examples that can be practiced within Python to help your knowledge grow and attain the best degree of understanding. Everything in this book has been verified and found accurate, which means that, if you run into a problem, you can always navigate back to the original examples to walk you through it. Definitions contained inside this book are accurately given through Python's website itself to improve reliability.

While there are multiple websites from which information was obtained, this book has compiled all steps and guidelines into an easy-to-read instructions that is as fun to practice as it is to read! *Learn Programming Python Like a Wizard: The Most Fun Python Course for Beginners* does not read like a manual, and completing the book is fast. While it is beneficial to learn definitions for any application you set your teeth into, slaving away in front of a device can become exhausting. That is why this book is designed with you in mind. We get it. It is hard to enjoy something that seems so complicated and muddled. The break down of basics should be fun and educational, which is what we aim for.

This book is an excellent guide into future programming endeavors. Easy navigation through the book is only one benefit to using this book. Often university classes move through programming quickly, so *Learn Programming Python Like a Wizard: The Most Fun Python Course for Beginners* is a great reference if you feel unsure of your programming career. This book is also set up to help parents teach children and teens to browse through if they are interested in programming. It is never too early to become interested in a quickly-growing industry.

Python is one of the easiest programming languages to learn, and it is no secret that it is one of the better-known platforms. Python provides commands that can be completed in minutes, and the results show quickly. Because it is so easy and manageable, Python is also an excellent gateway into other programming languages, which makes it one of the best programs to start to get your feet wet.

This book introduces topics such as installing Python, learning to interact with Python, basic functions, and more. While it is good to learn the definitions for any application you may start, it is set up to bring you to one of the most exciting parts of coding: actually programming within a system!

We have created a game in this book to bring all the concepts in this book together. Everyone wants to be a part of solving problems, and games may just be the best way to bring your knowledge of the software up to snuff. Through careful study, creating your own games, programs, libraries, and databases in Python will become easy and manageable for many years to come.

This book is designed with many fields in mind. Basically, that means that everything from sending mail to creating games in Python is laid out with step-by-step instructions to make learning easier. Think about what you want to do with Python. Are you looking to develop games? Are you more interested in creating databases for people who are willing to pay top dollar for you services? Are you more interested in creating libraries that will benefit others and start a freelancing gig of your own? Each of these career choices uses slightly different parts of the same application. If you are unsure of what you want to do for a potential job, the subjects in this book paint the way to several choices, all with people excited to work with you.

There are thousands of jobs available for those who know how to code. Many people who have programming occupations are not as skilled in it as you will be after you finish this book and practice the examples. The programming field is continually growing with each new addition of applications and features in the digital world. Python is an extremely adaptable programming software. Many people are interested in hiring someone to do the "heavy lifting," and programming is the way to get there.

So, with all of this information in mind, it only makes sense to get started with this book and make the most out of your programming journey. There is a lot to learn and so little time to do it! This book will guide you through the ins and outs of Python, which can create opportunities to experience life in a new career! Without further ado, let's dive deep into programming with *Learn Programming*

Python Like a Wizard: The Most Fun Python Course for Beginners!

Chapter 1: Why Learn to Code?

Coding is difficult and impossible to learn, right? After all, people go to school for four years to be qualified to create code. This myth has been circulating the internet since coding was conceptualized. Coding should not be any harder than learning another language, because that is what it is. Now, that may seem difficult, but there is one advantage Python has over any other language: it only takes an average of 6 - 8 weeks to master the basics.

There are plenty of excuses to not learn code, and many of them are perpetuated by myths from people both inside and outside the industry. Seeing a long list of Courier commands on a black screen may look daunting, but most coding is the repetition of simple commands that anyone can learn.

Common myths, such as "coding is too hard," prevent hard working people from exploring coding. Without proper motivation, it can be difficult to get in front of a computer screen and start pounding out codes. However, learning Python creates a fun and easy environment to start. But first, these myths

must be dispelled.

Myth: Coding is Hard to Learn

One of the reasons that most people believe that coding is difficult is because the only way to learn coding is through constant practice.

That means watching one video tutorial, as fun as it may be to watch YouTube and follow the instructions step by step, will not result in knowledge that sticks. Watching tutorials is a valuable asset to learning code, but sticking with code means testing basic commands. Once the basics are covered, there are many fun ways to play around with Python.

Web Development

Did you know that some of the internet community's favorite websites may operate thanks to Python? YouTube, Instagram, and Google are some of the websites that use Python. Web development is one of the major uses of Python, and its most popular. Since coding through Python is one of the simplest means to program, it remains the king of web development.

Web design is the culmination of a variety of basic functions. HTML and Javascript are two of the most basic web platforms, and once those are set up, Python is the language used to communicate with the database contained within basic website platforms. Python is the language that translate requests (called queries) into data output. Simple queries, like insert, delete, or modify, define how information is displayed, and becoming a master in the basics of Python makes data manipulation and web design so much easier.

Mobile Apps

Python is also a major contributor to the mobile world. Kivy and Beeware are the two most commonly used Python frameworks in use today. Both frameworks allow for a more desktop-like look to applications. This includes increased resolution in graphics that make for a more fun experience for users.

Mobile apps, like web development, use a stored database within the downloaded app to showcase information. Mobile phones now have much larger storage due to the information stored in each application. Python transforms code into displays that react based on information inputted. Each input by a user provides an equal output generated by the application. It is as simple as that.

Game Development

Developing games using Python is one of the best ways to get the most out of using Python. Because it is so easy to use, Python creates a platform that is useful in creating games. PyGame is one of the most popular ways to create games, and step-by-step guides are available to show you how to get there.

Artificial Intelligence (AI)

Robots are some of the most promising works of the future, and guess what? Robots can be designed using Python, one of the easiest coding languages to learn. Every part of a robot is controlled by small chips, which are easily programmable. Almost all coding done through Python for robots is completed in 30 lines or less, which means trial and error takes a lot less time.

Small projects, such as those involving Arduino and Raspberry Pi, take physical input with cables to the next level. Essentially, these interactive chips bridge the gap between coding and the physical world. A large number of these chips strung together create the bases for robots.

Coding is fun and very important for the future. Stories about the necessity of coding has circulated the internet for years, and it is only becoming more important as the years go by.

Myth: Coding is Boring

Humans have an innate nature to problem solve. It is why cathedrals, literary masterpieces, and science have evolved over the years. People from all walks of life have determined to create for convenience and beauty, since the dawn of time. Coding is a manifestation of this creation. Mechanical and artistic problems are solved through coding, and Python provides a way to connect physical objects with tangible results.

Creating line after line of coding with nothing but words displayed on the screen can seem boring. In fact, this is why most people avoid programming altogether. But, as discussed before, coding is far more than simply writing code. Coding is used for creation. Building a world through Minecraft is only the tip of the iceberg of what is possible in the world of coding. What is your passion?

Engineering and Mathematics

Engineering is the obvious choice for choosing coding. After all, an entire university major is devoted to creating artificial intelligence through programming chips to complete mundane and complex tasks. Python allows for easy problem solving using mathematics with graphical results. Python is common in engineering schools and is the gateway to other programming languages. Since it is easy to use, Python is also available for young people who want to get a leg up in the engineering field.

Art

Believe it or not, art is a common pastime for Python users. Pixelated pictures to oil painting-esk works are possible using Python. Since most people do not think of Python as a method to create art, creating pieces in the software is a challenge not easily solved. However, many websites and books are completely dedicated to artistic people.

Because creating within Python seems like a challenge, many people shy away from coding to follow pursuits that are easy (or easier) to accomplish. However, creating is just what Python was designed to do. Problem solving is ingrained in the human psyche. Coding may seem like a challenge at first, but once the basics are mastered, its convenience makes creation easily attainable, preparing coders for more challenges.

Myth: Coding is For Smart People

Oftentimes, people believe that coding is for people who are far smarter than the average person. Each person, however, has a unique way of seeing the world. No one is more or less clever than the next person, and everyone defines intelligence in different ways. Coding, therefore is the person who is willing to learn it. That means that brave people who can work logically are the perfect people to learn coding.

What does it mean to work logically? Well, consider this example. A salesperson working for a large business is assigned a task to create a graph showing the necessary changes in the sales department. Looking at statistics for the quarter, the saleperson may see an increase in overall chair sales, but the recliner has decreased in sales dramatically. The salesperson may see the decline as a consequence of lack of advertising and present it as such in the meeting. In essence, working logically is analyzing problems and coming up with solutions. It's just like programming work.

People who are able to think logically and come to conclusions about improvement are the perfect candidates for coding. This means that having a background in a scientific field may help in initial understanding, but most of the learning comes directly from adaptability.

It is a common myth that coding is only for people who major in a technical field or who have learned it from teachers before they are twenty are the only people who can master coding. In fact, most people have learned coding through reading books and attending online classes on websites such as Coursecа and Codeacademy (Larson, 2019). Effectively, most people have learned coding through how-to guides, like this one, that have helped them navigate through the basics. In other words, it does not take a fancy college degree to land a coding job.

People from across the globe are coding, which means that having a background in an industrial company does not disqualify anyone from learning. In fact, since Python is an application on a computer, most people only require a computer to get started. Libraries and local community centers have computers for those who do not have access at home. Most of these places also invite people who code to share experiences and help others learn to code.

Myth: Coding is For Guys

One of the most common misconceptions of coding is that it is only "for the guys." Men make up 80% of coders, mostly because they make up the majority of computer science classes in universities. Many people assume, because it is common to see men working in this field, that it is only *for* men. Women, however, are making strides to become more involved in STEM fields.

Girls Who Code, a not-for-profit organization focused solely on making STEM fields more accessible for women, is currently working to end stereotypes and help women become more interested and involved in coding. The organization provides resources such as classes on their website, clubs within both high schools and universities, and an online community to better help women teach themselves and each other. Though there may be plenty of developers who are men, but the playing field is changing, making room for more women in the workplace.

The computer science industry is booming, as is evident in both the news and social media. Not only is coding becoming easier to access, it is also becoming higher in demand. That is why starting children out in coding is a great head start for women in the industry. Parents who do not know how to get started can look to schools who provide places for young girls and women to learn.

Right now, only 25% of women are involved in coding in the workplace, but that could change for the better or worse. With so many jobs opening in the coding field, it is hard to believe that the number of women involved in coding is on the decline. Why? This generally because the industry is not seen as "cool." It is time to take coding to the next level. Involving girls within elementary schools gives children a thirst for creation. Problem solving, as discussed previously, is essential to human growth, and starting that process early ensures the coding industry can get some of the best people for the job, and that includes women.

Conclusion

Many believe that getting into coding is too hard or too much work, but just imagine what you can do with the knowledge! Coding takes diligence and hard work, but it is never too difficult for anyone. Python is unique because it is one of the least difficult languages to learn. Learning the basics is wildly beneficial, and it is through practice that the basics become the best asset of the coding world.

Coding does not have to be dreary; it can be as fun or as boring as you make it. There are thousands of applications you can use with Python, and that does not stop at mathematical subjects. Art programs allow for easy assimilation into the coding world for everyone interested in using a new medium.

Coding is not just for smart people, and it is not just for the guys. People who are willing to make an effort to learn coding will be surprised at how fast the learning process becomes. Being "smart" does not mean that you will not struggle. In fact, those who struggle the most are those who gain the most knowledge. Women from around the world are becoming more interested in computing jobs, and there are communities completely devoted to bringing in women, and their influence is some of the driving force behind much of coding today. It is vital to keep women interested in coding because of the perspectives and creativity they bring. Coding communities are always looking for women to join their teams.

Chapter 2: Our Digital World is a Fantasy World

What does that mean, anyway? The digital world includes anything the world imagines, and it keeps getting bigger. Communicating with the digital world is becoming wildly more important as the years go by. Many jobs are centered around software and internet usage. Some of these jobs are remote, allowing employees to work from home with more freedom and less unnecessary travel.

Coding is at the heart of this fantasy world. Whether using SQL, Python, or C++, developers are creating a world that is entirely dependent on virtual work. As the years go on, it is becoming vitally important to be a part of this world. Coding envisions and creates new mechanics to make life easier and more accessible. As dependence on virtual needs becomes more recognized, coding provides a way to take one step further in a successful future.

What is a Fantastic World?

What does a fantastic world mean? It means more than having a good life with friends on the beach. It means more than a wizard at school. When developing a fantasy world, characters and actions make the world what it is.

Some of the best fantasy novels use wizards, witches, and magic to create a world entirely different than this one. Magic creates a simpler life and achieves extraordinary tasks. Wizards and witches use this magic to accomplish tasks. Their skills allow them to make changes to their world with simple spells and incantations. The magic then translates that information into a result, be in physical or mental. A fantastic world is one in which saying simple words can change reality and matter. Do you see where this is going?

Coders are the magicians of this world. Using simple code, they can define what happens within a database to project information of any type. For example, consider a favorite game such as World of Warcraft or Minecraft. In that world, the player becomes part of the fantasy. Players can experience magic, crafting, and a wide variety of other simple and complex actions within the game. The game is part of a different world with its own rules and limitations. The fantasy world within these games is unique to every game and was designed, using code, to define the boundaries of the new world. The fantastic elements of another world may exceed the limits of reality, and each part of the game in which players participate is designed through coding.

How to Interact with This World

Coding is the key to unlocking a different world. Imagine a player within the game that has a decision to make, be that a challenge to complete or a turn to make. How does coding affect the outcome of the decision when each decision is different? Minute details within the system providing AND or OR responses coded inside the game determine the outcome. Excluding these stipulations prevents players from enjoying a more entertaining game.

For example, when a player in a racing game that includes driving along a straight line would be pretty boring. Now consider working in some turns and curves. This presents a whole new dilemma. Assuming the player drives along the curvy road with perfect precision, there are no consequences. However, if the road is curvy enough to make a player tumble off the road, what would happen? Results may conclude that the driver plummets off the road and he or she must restart the race, or the car may simply skid to a stop losing precious time on the result scores.

Now, consider a complication to the system. Not only do the results of going off the road affect the timer, but the game now introduces a second car into the mix. The second car can affect the car by winning, pushing the player's car off the road, or failing in such a way to affect the player. Suddenly, not only does the game include decisions about just driving down a road, there are now a multitude of complications that arise. Coding effectively creates the consequences of actions in the gaming system, giving the responses to a variety of actions that may occur during the game.

Web design is yet another part of a fantastic digital world. With the touch of a button, a customer can process an order, interact with interfaces on a page, and make choices based on the information found. To someone unfamiliar with working with the internet, it may appear that this is a work of magic, and the coder is the magician. To someone unfamiliar with coding, that might be an explanation as well. Coding is in the background of everything done on the internet and programmed into computers.

Why Do We Use This Comparison?

How much of the underlying happenings of technology is behind the scenes? Many people simply accept the fact that technology works. For example, many teenagers have mastered the selfie without knowing how the camera on the phone operates. Many more use social media to post pictures without understanding how Instagram or Facebook automatically places the photos online. The camera taking the picture uses light and its distributions to take a sample of whatever is focused in the lens. The aperture inside the lens then moderates how much light is transferred to the sensor. Finally, the picture is then saved within the phone's hardware. To someone who simply takes the photo, this may be magic, but that's where coders come in.

Coders define how a process completes. Coders know the ins and outs of how input corresponds to the output of data received from a database. Python's language automates the process of inputs to correspond to the same output. If this is confusing right now, don't worry. We will break it down using a robot as an example.

Imagine creating a robot that responds to light by closing a shade over its eyes. The written code explains what the robot must do when responding to light. A sensor in the robot's eyes processes the light which then sends information to the hardware located at the heart of this fictional robot. The inputted data then sends a response to the shutter to close the shade over the robot's eyes. As soon as the code is written and hardwired into the robot's heart, whenever exposed to light, the shutter will close over the robot's eyes.

Magic, right? Actually, through using basics in Python, coding can manipulate all parts of the robot. Problem solving through coding is one of the reasons that coding has advanced so far over the years. Once coding automates the actions of information input, future coding for the recommended output is unnecessary, and it behaves as though by magic. Coders, therefore, are the magicians, and coding is the magic.

What is Coding?

Coding is the means by which a database management system delivers information from the database. The coding language, such as Python, sends information requests to the database management system which then selects the information from the database and carries it back in the form of data. All languages of coding are designed to allow access through the database management system and to display in a manner convenient to the viewer. For those unfamiliar with these terms, we will dive more deeply into their meaning to make coding easier to understand.

First, a database is a place in which information is stored. That could mean numerical data or phrases. For example, suppose we build a website for an online bookstore. Each book is defined by a name, a page number, an author, and an arbitrary ordering number. If we use a relational database (which is all we are going to focus on in this book), all of that information is entered into a table. The columns define the types of sections in which the books can be displayed, which is name, page number, author, and that arbitrary ordering number. The rows in the table are filled with individual books and their information.

Next, the database management system (DBMS) does what its name implies: it manages the data within the database. The DBMS accesses any data within the database and feeds it back to the display. Data retrieved with the DBMS is commanded through a programming language called code.

Python is an example of this coding language, and the queries sent with code are translated using the DBMS which then accesses the information within the database. Data within the relational database must follow this order to display the correct information. Think of the process like a boomerang. When a query requesting information is processed, it must go through the DBMS, to the database, then back through the DBMS to show you the data on the computer screen.

Coding, therefore, is the means in which to manipulate data within a database to show information in an organized format. So, creating a game or developing a web display simply utilizes the coding in ways the user usually does not realize. Clicking on a button to purchase a book, for example, sends input into the database, marking it as SOLD and placing it into yet another table, perhaps named as books sold.

Why Learn Coding?

Most of the information in the last section probably seemed like a handful, but, once the basics are mastered, coding becomes extremely useful. Let us reflect on the online book store mentioned above. Without coding, the user would not be able to access the database. And, we will take this one step further, without coding, there would be no database for the customer to access! Without coding, the online book store would cease to exist.

Sure, coding is important to someone to keep the Internet running, but how should that affect the modern consumer who can pay to have it done? Coding allows for personal touches on websites and games (or anything) created. A coder can develop his or her own work to display new and creative products.

Developing code is also extremely useful in the job market. As the world is becoming more focused on computing, coders are necessary to create products for the rising generations. Companies such as Apple, Hewlett Packard, and many others depend on coding to enhance their products to cope with the ever-changing market. Programmers and developers from all over the world are in high demand to fill these positions.

Why Python?

With dozens of competing programming languages, why pick Python as the language of choice? Python has developed significantly over the years and has become one of the top programming languages in the world. Why? It is simple to understand and operate, and it is a high-level programming language that is easy to understand. Python allows for more fulfilling work in fewer steps.

Python provides background for many support libraries. Libraries are inherently programmed into a coding language. Python uses libraries with areas in string operations, web service tools, Internet, protocols, and operating system interfaces. (Mindfire Solutions, 2017). This means that Python is already supported with these operations, making programming that much easier.

Python also increases overall productivity by providing integrations with other programming languages such as C++ and Java. Simple interaction with each language gives Python a leg up from other coding languages. Python creates services that work quickly and efficiently and are the basis for many multi-protocol applications.

Services, such as Google, use Python as their primary programming language, and many others are using its extensive library background and easy coding structure to build competitive coded designs. So, if coders are interested in building a foundation for large companies, Python provides an advantage that other languages lack. Familiarity with its background boosts resumes for potential job seekers.

While Python is one of the top programming languages in the world, it does not yet have some of the capabilities of other technologies such as JDBC and ODBC. However, Python gives the background necessary to understand other coding languages. Python is continually improving to become a top competitor in these other technologies. Because it is the frontrunner of many online and software packages, it continues to improve as the years go by.

Conclusion

The world inside Python is like a fantasy world. You can create anything you wish in Python, and that ranges from games to business software. Python offers an excellent background for anyone interested in programming because many programming languages have many of the same basic codes. Python can hold its own in the programming world, and it is free, so beginning a life of programming with Python is a great option.

Interacting with Python comes through many series of threads, creating a base for this world. Just as an author may create a world through words, so programming creates the visual world through its language: code. Coding is a series of definitions, commands, and computer genius to process information and make changes in our digital world.

As the world becomes more computerized, it is becoming more vital to know the basics of how this world works. Python is one of the most utilized programming basis on the internet and for private applications. Python has a highly functional computer basis. This means that it can do a wide variety of tasks, and it contains a large background for continual growth.

Chapter 3: Installing Python

One of the greatest perks of using Python is its affordability. Schools usually offer Python at a discounted rate, and some sites even offer the program free of charge. The Pycharm community offers Python free of charge for those who do not want the full features of the product. These simplified features still allow coders to use basic coding, but it does not offer the full benefits of web development, scientific tools, or database and SQL tools. If you are serious about starting your own business using coding through Python, the professional version is the best option.

Windows

Installing Python on Windows is easy and usually does not take long, but this is highly dependent on internet speed. Python is not inherently located on Windows computers, so it is necessary to follow the steps for download. Pycharm's website is set up with various types of downloads suited to any type of computer and processing type. However, new models with higher processing speeds are preferred.

System Requirements

To install Python on a Windows computer, there are a few qualifications to keep in mind. Be aware of your computer's capabilities. Though it is possible to download software that just qualifies for installation, it may not perform to appropriate standards. Just as downloading an app on a flip mobile phone would be quite a feat, so would downloading Python in conditions that it is ill fit to process.

Downloading Python on an old computer is difficult and often results in a failed download. To prevent failed downloads or slow processing times, it is best to keep the system requirements provided by Pycharm in mind.

System Version
Microsoft Windows 10, 8, and 7 are the versions preferred when downloading Python. 64-bit versions of Windows are also preferred,

but not necessary. 32-bit versions are more than welcome when downloading Python on a Windows computer, and it will not slow down processes, though it may not have all the features of the 64-bit version. Python also supports Windows XP, but explore which version is best for your computer before download.

RAM and Disc Space
Obviously, as with any application, the more RAM and disc space, the faster the processing time. Python recommends a 4 GB RAM and 1.5 GB hard disk space with at least 1 GB for additional caches on a desktop for optimal processing, but anything larger than that is highly preferred. Python also suggests a 1024 x 768 screen resolution minimum to make the most out of the program.

Installation

Because there are various Windows models and versions, we will break down the downloading process for each. Feel free to skip to the download version most suitable for your computer.

Windows 10, 8, or 7

Though there are prereleases available for a majority of Python versions, the best bet is to download a stable copy. Python suggests a version of 2.7, 3.5, or newer. The newest stable copy is available at jetbrains.com/pycharm which shows up as a large black button at the top of the page. The button redirects to a page which gives two options: Professional or Community. Download a copy using the following instructions.

1. Select the version Professional or Community to begin download. Note that Community is the free option.
2. Run the file or select the downloading box in the bottom left corner once it has completed the download.
3. Select **Next** to continue.
4. Define the destination folder or let Pycharm define it for you and select **Next**.
5. Check the option to create a shortcut, update context menu, create associations, update PATH variable, or check nothing then select **Next**.
6. Select a **Start** menu folder in which to retrieve Python. JetBrains is already selected.
7. Install.
8. Select **Finish**.

9. Download Python at the Windows app store for Python's IDLE.

Navigate to Python using the search bar for Windows 10 and 8, and find Python in File Explorer on Windows 7. Download all files associated with Pycharm.

Windows XP
Because Python is becoming more sophisticated, older versions of Windows generally do not support the new versions of Python. Pycharm allows for the download of Python 2.7.10, which is the newest version supported by Windows XP. If you are not sure if 32-bit or 64-bit is correct for your computer, select 32-bit (or x86), just to be on the safe side. However, downloading on Pycharm should accommodate your computer's specifications. Install a copy using the following directions.

1. Select the version Professional or Community to begin download. Note that Community is the free option.
2. Find the file listed as **pycharm-community-(version number)-(windows version).msi.**
3. Double click on the file and allow any requested permissions from Windows.
4. Install **Pycharm** when the window opens.

5. Agree to the licensing agreement.
6. Do not select any customization for Python.
7. Install.
8. Select **Finish**.
9. Download Python at the Windows app store for Python's IDLE.

To find the file, navigate to Start, select All Programs, and find Pycharm as one of the installed applications. Download all files related to Pycharm. Once open, type in the code `print("Hello, World!")`. If you received `Hello, World!` as a response, your installation was successful.

Linux

Windows and Mac seem like the forerunners in the computing game. They have both been around for years and they are heavily user friendly. Linux, however, has been around for many years and is one of the most popular operating systems around the world. Unlike Mac and Windows, Linux offers a platform that directly instigates communicates between the hardware and software. And, it is one of the most secure operating systems on the planet. It is not uncommon for computers to perform for years without a reboot (Linux.com). Because it is free to download, many computers now opt for this additional package, which is why Python is a common addition to its software.

Linux is also unique in its ability to work with different Python packages. Because the operating system is designed to directly integrate a computer's hardware with its software, it is easier to configure some projects in Linux than it is in the other operating systems. Finally, most of coding with Python downloaded on a computer is done locally, but Linux allows a public view. That means that a majority of projects available to the public must be done in a Linux system, making it helpful to learn this platform.

System Requirements

Python on Linux is possible for most major OS system, but there are system requirements set aside by Pycharm to insure a computer can handle the processes of Python coding. Linux is designed with different packages to adhere to coders starting off and those who have worked in the system for some time. As such, there are limitations of bit distribution, RAM, and hard disk space. Find out what capabilities your computer has through accessing system specifications through the search window on your computer.

Bit Distribution
According to Pycharm, Python works best with a 64-bit Linux distribution with any of the distribution packages including Gnome, KDE, or Unity. However, this does not mean that a 32-bit package is unsuitable for download. Again, be aware of your computer's processing speed. If you are unsure of which to download and are not looking for large packages, simply install the 32-bit package. It is always possible to download the largest version later.

RAM and Disk Space
Just like any computer, if the hard drive is full, it is unlikely that operations will move smoothly. Now, imagine working ten programs with limited disk space and small RAM packages. Those programs will never have a chance. Therefore, Pycharm suggests a 4 GB minimum in RAM, though more is always better. Linux also requires 1.5 GB of hard disk space with an additional 1 GB for caches. Again, when it comes to programming within

your system, it is always best to leave additional space.

Installation

Unlike either Windows or Mac, Linux may have Python already installed in its software. Its Red Hat Package Manager (RPM) already has the installation, and, in that case, the installation is already complete. In this case, installation is simple. However, if Python does not exist on Linux, follow these simple instructions to install Python.

Standard Linux Installation

The standard Linux installation works with any system and is the most basic form of installation. However, it does require input commands to complete. Interfacing with the system is required to complete the installation. Pycharm provides a link to other Linux installations to give you the best version.

1. Navigate to jetbrains.com/python for installation.
2. Select **Download** or **Other Versions** to find the correct version for your computer.

3. Select Save when the popup for requested actions appears.
4. Double click the downloaded file and find it within folder.
5. Open a terminal.
6. Type **sudo apt-get install build-essential** and press enter to install the Builds Essential Support.
7. Type **sudo apt-get install libsqlite3-dev** to install SQLite Support.
8. Type **sudo apt-get install libbz2-dev** to get Linux's required file to access Python.
9. Copy **pycharm-(date of latest version).tar.gz** and place in the appropriate folder. Note that RW permissions are necessary to change the location.
10. Unpack the downloaded file using the command **tar -xzf pycharm-(date of latest version).tar.gz**

Graphical Installation

Occasionally, larger packages of Linux require the graphical installation of Python. Ubuntu is a common package for Python installation, and thus will be included in these instructions. However, others are similar to Ubuntu.

1. Open Ubuntu Software Center.
2. Select Development Tools from the All Software dropdown menu.
3. Double click on Python.

4. Install.

To navigate to Python, run pycharm.sh from the bin subdirectory. Download all files related to Pycharm and its community. To see if it works, enter the code `print("Hello, World!")`. If you receive `Hello World!` as a response, you have successfully completed the installation.

Mac

Mac, like the other platforms, provides highly accessible interactions with Python, and it may already be installed on your computer. However, most Python applications are out of date on the Mac, and using Pycharm to download the most recent version of Python gets you the best of what Python can offer. For Mac users, installation is different than the others. Downloading the Xcode Command Line Tools and Homebrew are both necessary before Python. First, though, Mac also has requirements for it installation.

System Requirements

For optimal results when downloading the latest version of Python, Mac requires basic standards. Since there are variations of Python available for virtually any operating system, including mobile devices, requirements such as disc space, RAM, and 32-bit / 64-bit operate differently for each system. Find the specifications of your device before choosing the type of download that is most helpful for you. Pycharm has a community of users that share information and give out handy tricks, and it is the method we will use to install Python.

Bit Distribution

As we mentioned earlier, there are generally two types of bit distributions in the forms of 32- and 64-bit versions of MacOS. If you are still on an older version of Mac, it is best to update if you want the latest version. Python has options available for older devices, but why not get the latest and greatest version of Python? If you are unsure about what bit distribution is right for you, consider what uses you will get out of the software. Beginners may only need the 32-bit distribution, as it is more than equipped to handle the basics. Later on, downloading the 64-bit version may be the best option when you have moved to more advanced features.

RAM and Disk Space
Like both Linux and Windows, Pycharm requirements to use the most recent version, but more disc space and RAM will speed projects along and allow for more saved features. Pycharm recommends a 4 GB RAM and 1.5 GB hard disk space with an additional 1 GB for caches at a minimum. More RAM and disc space allows for quicker processes. Find your computer's capabilities to find out how much space can be devoted to Python functions.

Installation

Python installation on a Mac is slightly more complex than it is on either a Windows or Linux operating system. Additional installations of Xcode and Homebrew are necessary to handle Python operations. Luckily, both are easily installed using the Apple app store.

Xcode and Homebrew

Both the application Xcode and its tools are necessary for Mac to translate code correctly. First, download Xcode by going to the Apple app store. It may take some time to download because it is fairly big, so you might need to grab a sandwich in the meantime. Once completed, install the Apple command line tools under the Xcode menu. Select Preferences and install from there.

To download Homebrew use the following code in an open terminal: `ruby -e "$(curl -fsSL` `https://raw.github.com/mxcl/homebrew/go)`. Consider the terminal as a place for code. If you are unfamiliar with it, you may have seen it during the installation of Xcode. It is also seen as a folder where all processes are taking place. Generally Homebrew will help you with the remaining parts of the installation.

Once completed, you can download the latest version of Python by writing the code `brew install python`. The newest version of Python has then been installed.

Python Installation

Pycharm offers an easy installation that follows the same process as both Windows and Linux. Other installations and types are available on the website by selecting Other Versions. Pick the version that is most suited to your computer. Install Python by following the directions below.

1. Navigate to jetbrains.com/pycharm.
2. Select the black button labeled Download.
3. Select one of the options listed for Professional or Community download. Note that the Community download is free. The options on the left navigate to other installations.
4. Select the file marked pycharm-(date of recent release).dmg, which is a disk image file.
5. Select it as another program or disk added to the system.
6. Send Pycharm to the Applications folder through copying.

Download all files related to Pycharm and its community. And that's it! That is the installation processes for all three operating services mentioned here. Simple, right?

Conclusion

Installing Python should not be a hassle. This chapter went over the processes to download Python in detail, so, if you ever wonder how to download it again, fall back on this chapter.

Windows, Linux, and Mac recommend the latest version of Python, but that does not mean that the 64-bit application is necessary for better graphics or coding within Python. Choose the right download is the best for your computer. Remember that 32-bit is more than enough for learning Python.

Though you can choose any version of Windows, Linux, or Mac, it is always best to choose the latest. Pycharm's website provides multiple versions and a community on which to lean if you feel like you do not have enough support.

Chapter 4: Python's Basics

Now that installation is complete, we can continue to the fun of programming! For absolute beginners, this chapter provides the absolute basics of Python terminology. Because Python is one of the most beginner-friendly programming languages, it also paves the way for introductions into other programming languages. Its simplicity also allows for faster learning and quicker results when you start coding like a pro.

All programming languages require an Integrated Development Environment (nicknamed "IDLE"). IDLE has both a text editor and a shell; the shell is what you see when you enter Python, and the text editor is designed to create the environment in which to create, delete, or update data (Variables & Data Types). Python, luckily, has its own IDLE built into the system. No extra installation needed. The basics, therefore, are all we need to get started with coding in Python.

Variables

A variable is defined as a series of letters that hold some value within the database. Just as you may see in mathematics, variables do not include numbers, dashes, underscores, or spaces. Python variables are case sensitive, so using a capital letter in as a defined variable means that the variable is permanently listed

with a capital letter in the database.

Exercise: Hello World!

In the previous chapter, `print("Hello World!")` was the test code to make sure everything installed correctly. Now, with the use of x as the variable, we will define x as *Hello World!*

```
x = "Hello World!"
print(x)
```

With the newly defined x, memory has been set aside to define future coding with x as *Hello World!* Since *Hello World!* is not a variable in the way that x is defined as such, Python has reconfigured the variable into a text string. The second line in the script prints the variable x, which has been redefined. In effect, the code `print(x)` will now be processed as the literal text for variable x.

```
print("Hello World!")
```

Exercise: Nickname

Defining a variable in Python is also useful in creating shortcuts. In this exercise you will create a nickname for yourself and define it using variables. First, define three variables for your first name, last name, and nickname. `fname`, `n_name`, and `lname` are the defined variables. We place Sammy in parentheses to show that it is a nickname.

```
fname = "Sam"
n_name = "(Sammy)"
lname = "Jones"
print (fname + " " + n_name + " " + lname)
```

The print above contains quotation marks in the print command because it includes spaces. Since fname, n_name, and lname have already been defined, they do not require quotation marks. The resulting code gives the first name, nickname in parenthesis, and last name defined.

```
Sam (Sammy) Jones
```

Data Types

Python has a wide variety of data types that define how information is stored. Python has many data types, which include integers, floats, boolean, and strings (Heba, 2019). Variables were discussed first because they are how data is stored. Different types of data respond differently within Python, and simple letters are the tip of the iceberg.

Integers and Floats

Numbers are essential to Python's makeup, and they are stored as numbers. Integers within Python are defined by "int." Floats are numbers defined by standard notation. For example, a float for 10,845,836 may be 1.085+E7, effectively putting the large number into standard notation. Numbers in Python may also include complex, negative, positive, or long numbers.

Each of these numbers can be manipulated in Python to show different results. For example, defining `complex (x, y)` in Python will conclude with two parts of a number, one real and the other imaginary. A number that has been shortened in Python to allow easier readability is expanded through the change in definition `long (x)`. If the integer is too long, Python will only show a certain number and then finish with an L.

Boolean and String

A string is a list of characters and are represented by "str." Stings can be words or phrases and are always accompanied by quotation marks. "This is a string" is an example of a coded string. Booleans, shortened to "bool" within Python, give true or false answers only.

Operations

Operations insert, change, or delete data. They are the essence of data manipulation. Previously, we defined several simple operations within Python regarding variables and viewed the results. Operations can be as simple as defining a variable, or they can become more complex, like ordering a sensor to take a sample of soil toxicity. Here, however, we will start with simple operations.

Operators

Operators such as addition, subtraction, multiplication, and division are the bread and butter of Python, just as they are with mathematics. Operators combine the same data types together and are used with most data types. The operators most common in Python are the following.

"+"   Addition

"-"   Subtraction

"*"   Multiplication

"/"   Division

"**"   Exponential

"//"   Integer division

"%"   Modulus (which gives the remainder of a division)

The rules of operations apply when using all operators. For those who have forgotten the order, it is included below.

1. Parentheses
2. Exponents
3. Multiplication/Division

4. Addition/Subtraction

The union of operators need not include numbers. Strings are also commonly connected using these operators. As was seen previously in the variable example regarding entering a nickname, adding strings together produce a phrase. Integers and strings, however, will not combine due to their data types.

Print ( )

The `print( )` operator, which is used to display completed operations, is how Python responds to code. Operations involving boolean, integer, strings, and floats all receive output from the `print( )` function. For example, using a complex operation to find all the prime numbers between some interval requires multiple lines of code. To see the finished result, the `print( )` function must appear at the end of the line. When defining variables by using strings, multiplying a word by three is only viewed through using the `print( )` function.

Conditionals

Conditionals refer to results that yield true or false responses. In other words, conditionals return boolean responses. These results are only possible if certain criteria are met. Therefore, they must involve comparisons. Operations without comparisons yield results with operations like those of those listed above.

Comparison Operators

Comparison operators are self-explanatory: they compare data with other data. Mathematics uses comparison operators frequently. Consider two companies whose product sales are comparable. If Company A has a larger selection of the product than Company B, it is logical to assume that the number of products sold for Company A are greater than or equal to those of Company B. Comparison operators use this logic to create conditions for operations. The list of comparison operators are listed below.

"<"   Less than

"$>$"   Greater than

"$<=$"   Less than or equal to

"$>=$"   Greater than or equal to

"$==$"   Equal to

"$!=$"   Not equal to (Sturtz, 2019)

All comparison operators compare boolean data types, but only the "$==$" and "$!=$" are possible for numbers and strings ("Conditions").

Functions

Unlike mathematical functions, one operation does not always yield an answer. Block functions create several lines of code to produce one result. This does not mean that a function cannot be determined from a single line, but Python makes it unnecessary to receive an answer for every line only to continue the same code structure on the next. For example, a block of code may involve only a simple operation and print clause. Functions offer faster reaction time and allow coders to get more done in a shorter amount of time.

Parameters for functions are located within the definition clause inside parentheses. These could be as simple as the variable *x*, or they could define a term used throughout the function. Arguments are the inputs into a functions. Examples of these may include `def( )` or `greet( )`, though there are plenty of others Python has already stored, and many others that coders can add along the way.

The return value marks a function complete. When it is expressed in a function, it is accompanied by an expected result such as True or False. As you may have guessed, these are popular for boolean data types. However, it is not always necessary to use the return value. For example, in the variable exercises, return was not used as a determining factor for the completed function. After the definition of *x* changed to *Hello, World!*, we simply used the `print( )` function to complete it.

Regular Expressions (Regex)

Regular expressions are those already listed within Python. They need no definition for use within the program. The Regex model links two strings together through matching characters. For example, a regular expression may be defined within Python as "search," and the characters may match those inputted into Python as "search."

Creating connections between characters entered within Python may define conditions. For example, if A is defined as a regular expression and B has the same characters as A, they can also be defined as AB. If A is linked to R, B is linked to Z, and A and B are linked, so must R and Z. There are, however, exceptions to this rule. If a metacharacter changes the meaning of a regular expression or causes repetition, regular expressions will yield poor results. Characters such as ., ^, \$, *, +, ?, (,), [, and] are examples of these metacharacters.

"." The dot matches every character except a new line and DOTALL matches every character regardless of the new line.

"^" The carat matches every start of the string.

"$" The dollar sign matches the end of every string.

"?" The question mark catches repetitions of the previous regular expressions.

"\" The dash allows you to escape any special characters, like the question mark.

"[ ]" The brackets show characters in a sequence. Ranges and individual sequences are possible inside brackets. They can be listed as [abc] or [a-c].

". . ." The ellipsis continues a function and refers to the information listed in parentheses (Python).

Read / Write File

Python is remarkably handy with its read/write files. Unlike many other programming languages, Python already has built in functions, and, if it does not have what you are looking for, there are multiple files that

Pycharm provides that will help you with the process.

Python characterizes its file types as either text or binary, and it is important to know the difference. Binary is computer language, which, unless you are fluent from spending hours staring at it, is really confusing for the average Joe. Binary displays in 0s and 1s in various orders to create characters that are recognizable to people. For example, the number 9 in binary is 110100, and it becomes far more confusing for larger numbers and strings. Text libraries hold files that are more recognizable to humans. It displays binary into the code seen in Python.

Reading a File

There are several ways to read a file within Python, but we will stick to the basics. The command `file.read( )` extracts characters from a string. When writing the code within Python, the code looks something like this.

```
file = open("randomfile.txt")
print(file.read( ))
```

What if, however, you want to get more specific than that? Python has specific code to extract certain characters or lines within a code by refining the code above. Say, for example, we want to look for the first twelve characters within a code to start off a sequence. The code would read the following.

```
file = open("randomfile.txt")
print(file.read(12))
```

If we use the previous Hello World! example, the first characters would read just that: *Hello World!* When looking for an entire line in a file, its code would read as follows:

```
file = open("randomfile.txt")
print(file.readline( ))
```

The resulting information from the file would reveal all information from the line specified.

Writing a File

Just as inputting data into Python only requires inserting code, so writing within a file is just inputting data within the text file. Writing a file only includes one parameter, so this section will be small. First a file must be open to write code inside.

```
file = open("randomfile.txt")
file.write("This is random text")
file.write("Another sentence")
file.close("randomfile.txt")
```

This last line completes the sequence, closing the file and allowing for code entry outside the file.

Conclusion

As we have mentioned before, becoming a master at the basics is the best way to get to know the language better and create a background for more advanced applications. If you have not mastered the basics, it is unwise to move on from this chapter. Take the time to really know how to process information in Python.

Variables help you define objects and functions within Python. Without them, saving important information is impossible. Variables are defined through certain data types, and data types must not be intermingled. Strings, integers, floats, and boolean are the most common types of data.

Operators, such as those that define mathematical functions, are essential to completing functions within Python. The mathematical operators in Python are used for strings and boolean, too. They combine or detract from data. Conditionals, along the same vein, act as comparison devices, defining inequalities within functions. Unlike operators, conditionals are only useful with integer results. The functions that operators and conditionals create can be stored within Python and used at a later date. These functions are a continued line of code dependent on the operation of each equation within the thread.

Regular expressions link strings together by matching signs outside the same code line. Links are essential in Python to code properly. Setting a file to read / write makes it easier to access in the future, and it is necessary to change information.

Chapter 5: Object-Oriented Programming

Object-oriented programming (OOP) is a programming paradigm designed to track real objects through a detailed structure based on properties. This model classifies objects based on literal characteristics such as physical characteristics, behavioral characteristics, or number of objects. The OOP model keeps the descriptions of real objects in a readable format that is easily accessible through entering code in Python.

For example, consider a zoo. Some of the characteristics noted in the program may include the number of animals contained within the facility. It may also contain the behavioral characteristics of the elephants, exercise the giraffe gets, and the amount of water inside the hippopotamus pen. These characteristics are set into a table that is accessed through Python. When a chimpanzee, for example, needs to update his medication, Python creates a program to fit that characteristic for future access.

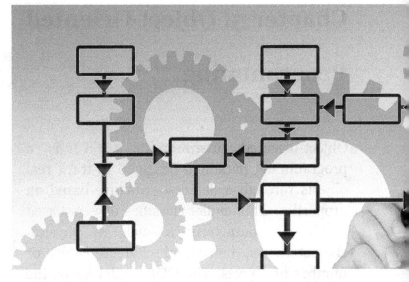

In another example, a company needs to take care of its produce. The entries into Python may express the date of last purchase, the number of apples in inventory, and the overall sales from produce. This list of data needs updating frequently, and Python's programming paradigm organizes the information for easy access within the software.

The Concepts of OOP

OOP contains some basic concepts that define information put into the programming paradigm. The different classifications include method, inheritance, polymorphism, data abstraction and encapsulation. Each break down information to make it more readable within Python. Since OOP in also available in other programming languages, learning these concepts makes crossover easier.

Method

Methods are similar to functions within Python, but they are not quite the same. Methods only work within classes. This means that, though they behave like functions, they only work when defined within a class. There are two types of methods: those that work directly within a class and those that work with class instances.

Methods within classes are functions specified to the class. In other words, functions that contain many lines within a class are defined as methods. The data retrieved from the class (which is the blueprint for adding data) can only be manipulated through methods. An instance is essentially an object, and many use them interchangeably. So, a method within a class instance does not depend on long lines associated with the whole table within Python, but rather only one object.

Inheritance

One of the most essential parts of Python is its capability for inheritance. Just as inheritance means relating an object or characteristic from parent to child, so inheritance within Python means handing down classifications from parent classification to child classification. For example, envision a used car dealership. It may contain cars, boats, or motorcycles. Each of these classes can pass down their characteristics to the vehicles on the lot. A car, for instance, may require further breaking down to trucks, sedans, and hatchbacks. These cars share the characteristics of the car classification, which they inherited. These are called subclasses. The code for this example may read as follows.

```
class Sedan(Cars)
```

The sedans in the car lot now share the classifications of cars on the lot. A list of attributes obviously follows.

Polymorphism

Polymorphism's literal meaning is "many forms." As covered previously in inheritance, the child form inherits its attributes from its parent. But what happens when the method in the parent's classification does not quite fit that of the child? This process is called method override. Polymorphism allows a child within a parent/child relationship to change some of the methods inherited from the parent.

Bringing back the example at the used car dealership, what if a classification of "boat" does not fit the child's definition of boat. Perhaps the boat is actually a houseboat, so it does not have jet propulsion or sails. How would we classify this object then? The method override sequence allows for an addendum to some of the methods within the "boat" class. The following code is an example of how a method override may appear.

```
class Boat:
        def explore(self)
```

```
        print("explore(   )   method  from  class
Boat")
class Houseboat(Boat)
        def explore(self)
        print("explore(   )   method  from  class
Houseboat"
Houseboat_propulsion = Houseboat( )
Boat_propulsion = Boat( )
Houseboat_propulsion.explore( )
Boat_propulsion.explore( )
```

The method override completes the code and allows for change to the houseboat rules, which, in turn, changes the information that led to its classification.

Data Abstraction and Encapsulation

Data abstraction and encapsulation are used synonymously because encapsulation is the method by which data abstraction is achieved. When data within a method is purposefully designed to be untouched, encapsulation prevents data changes outside the method. Correct values are essential in methods, so this system prevents errors.

When defining objects within a method, underscores determine whether an object can be retrieved. No underscore defines a variable, but it is possible to change it outside the method. One underscore defines a variable but puts in a private setting. This means that only those within the method can access the variable. A variable with two underscores prevents changes to the variable outside the method, and it is more difficult to change it within the method as well, though it is possible. An error will occur if the variable is expected to print outside the method. Data abstraction is achieved within the method using the double underscore definition.

Example: How to Create an Object "Wizard"

Now that we have seen the basics of OOPs, we will get to the fun part: creating a wizard within the system. It is important that you understand the abstract processes of OOP concepts above before you get started. First we will define some of the characteristics of the wizard: name, life point, manna point, attack point, def point, dodge point, and potion.

```
import random
class Wizard:
        def    __init__(self,    name,    life_pt,
mana_pt, atk_pt, def_pt, dodge_pt, potion):
```

```
        self.name = name
        self.life_pt = life_pt
        self.mana_pt = mana_pt
        self.atk_pt = atk_pt
        self.def_pt = def_pt
        self.dodge_pt = dodge_pt
        self.potion = potion
```

With that code completed, the next step is defining the method.

```
    def wizardAttack(self, lp_dragon):
        print("Wizard's attack")
        return lp_dragon - self.atk_pt
    def wizardDefense(self, attack_dragon):
        if random.randint(1, 6) > 4:
            print("Defend          yourself
!!")
            return     self.def_pt     -
attack_dragon
        else:
            print("Ouch  you  take  it
!!")
            return attack_dragon

    def wizardDodge(self, attack_dragon):
        if random.randint(1, 6) > 4 and
self.dodge_pt > 0:
            print("You dodge it")
            self.dodge_pt -= 100
        else:
            print("Dodge failed !!")
            return attack_dragon
    def tackPotion(self):
        if self.potion > 0:
            print("-------------->")
            print("Take potion")
            print("------------->")
            self.life_pt += 500
            self.potion -= 1
        else:
            print("You  have  no  more
potions")
    def launchSpell(self):
```

84

```
        print("-------------->")
        print("Launch fates")
        print("-------------->")
        self.atk_pt += 1000
        self.mana_pt -= 100
    def showStat):
        print("               ------
-Wizard Stats-------")
        print("
Life point " + str(self.life_pt))
        print("
Mana point " + str(self.mana_pt))
        print("
Attack point " + str(self.atk_pt))
        print("
Defense point " + str(self.def_pt))
        print("
Dodge point " + str(self.dodge_pt))
        print("              ------
----------------------")
```

How to Create an Object "Dragon"

Next, we will define a dragon to add to the mix. Since we have created the wizard in our game to attack the dragon, it only makes sense to create a dragon for him or her to fight. The same principles apply when creating the dragon. Since the game involves their fight, life points, mana points, attack points, def points, and dodge points are all necessary to have a game worth playing.

The method for completing these actions within the code are defined by the dragon's attack, defence, and dodge. Each of these must be defined for them to work in the game.

```python
import random
class Dragon:
    def __init__(self, life_pt, mana_pt, atk_pt, def_pt, dodge_pt):
        self.life_pt = life_pt
        self.mana_pt = mana_pt
        self.atk_pt = atk_pt
        self.def_pt = def_pt
        self.dodge_pt = dodge_pt
    def dragonAttack(self, lp_wizard):
        print("Dragon's Attack")
        if random.randint(1, 6) > 4:
            print("Wizard is hit !!!")
            return lp_wizard - self.atk_pt
        else:
            print("Attack failed !!!")
            return lp_wizard
    def dragonDefense(self, attack_wizard):
        if random.randint(1, 6) > 4:
            print("Dragon defends")
            return self.def_pt - attack_wizard
        else:
            print("Dragon is hit!!")

            return attack_wizard
    def dragonDodge(self, wizard_atk):
        print("Dragon tries to dodge")
        if random.randint(1, 6) > 4 and self.dodge.pt > 0:
            print("Dragon dodges")
            self.dodge_pt -= 50
            return 0
        else:
            print("Dodge failed !!")
            return wizard_atk
    def dragonChoice(self):
```

```
            return str(random.randint(1, 3))
        def showStat(self):
            print("                         ------
-Dragon Stats--------")
            print("
        Life point " + str(self.life_pt))
            print("
        Mana point " str(self.mana_pt))
            print("
        Attack point " + str(self.atk_pt))
            print("
        Defense point " + str(self.def_pt))
            print("
        Dodge point " + str(self.dodge_pt))
            print("                         ------
--------------------")
```

Python's Classes and Objects

Both objects and classes are the basics of data structures. Each of them define classifications for data within Python. Objects are the basis for starting the blueprint within Python. Most programming languages create virtual tables in which to hold various data, and Python is no exception. Objects define the data within the database and classes are part of the programming paradigm to set up reachable actions.

87

Objects

Objects are the most basic form of classification within Python. Each object has its own characteristics, which may be both physical and behavioral. Multiple names and characteristics can belong to each object. For example, an elephant in the zoo may contain both physical and behavioral characteristics that are unique to it. A white spot or an anger issue may characterize this elephant.

Classes

Unlike objects, classes within Python are completely used for structure. Creating attributes for one object is easy within Python, but without proper structure, adding other objects and their attributes to the program may become confusing. Classes define characteristics by their names and put them into categories. Though classes may contain information regarding objects, they offer no information in and of themselves (Real Python, 2019). They provide only a layout in which information can be organized.

For instance, adding an elephant to code requires knowledge of its attributes. Since an elephant is classified as a mammal, its definition will include that classification.

```
class: Elephant
       species = "mammal"
```

So, when creating a class for animals within the zoo, the elephant will be included in the mammal class. If called upon for all elephants, they will read as mammals.

Solve Python Problems Using OOP

Now that you have gotten a taste of OOP processing, it is time to solve problems associated with the terminology you just learned. The problems listed here are supplied by Real Python.

Exercise: Dog Inheritance

Problem

Create a code that reads the following lines:

```
I have 2 dogs.
Liza is 7.
Peter is 13.
They are all classified as mammals.
```

Solution

When creating code, the "#" sign creates a line that is not part of the regular text. This is useful when explaining code within a method. The following "#" signs will define what is happening in the code. The following code will produce the output listed above.

```python
#Parent class
class Dog:

    #Class attribute
    species = "mammal"

    #Initializer / Instance attributes
    def __init__(self, name, age):
        self.name = name
        self.age = age

    #Instance method
    def description(self):
        return "{ } is { } years old".format(self.name, self.age)

    #Instance method
    def speak(self, sound):
```

```
            return    "{    }    says    {    }"
.format(self.name, sound)

#Child class (inherits from Dog class)
class Labrador(Dog):
    def run(self, speed):
            return    "{    }    runs    {    }"
.format(self.name, speed)

#Child class (inherits from Dog class)
class AustralianCattleDog(Dog):
    def run(self, speed):
            return "%s runs %s" % (self.name,
speed)

#Create instances of dogs
my_dogs = [
    Labrador("Liza", 7),
    AustralianCattleDog("Peter", 13)
]

#Instantiate the Pets class
my_pets = Pets(my_dogs)

#Output
print("I    have    {    }    dogs."
.format(len(my_pets.dogs)))
for dog in my_pets.dogs:
    print("{ } is { }.".format(dog.name,
dog.age))


print("They are all classified as { }s."
.format(dog.species)) (Real Python, 2018)
```

Exercise: My Dogs are Hungry

Problem

Create a code that reads the following lines:
```
```

```
I have 2 dogs.
Liza is 7.
Peter is 13.
They are all classified as mammals.
My dogs are hungry.
```

Solution

The following code will produce the output listed above.

```python
#Parent class
class Pets:
        dogs = [ ]
        def __init__(self, dogs):
                self.dogs = dogs

#Parent class
class Dog:
        #Class attribute
        species = "mammal"

        #Initializer / Instance attributes
        def __init__(self, name, age):
                self. name = name
                self.age = age

        #Instance method
        def description(self):
                return self.name, self.age

        #Instance method
        def speak(self, sound):
                return "% says %s" % (self.name,
sound)

        #Instance method
        def eat(self):
                self.is_hungry = False

#Child class (inherits from Dog class)
class Labrador(Dog):
```

```python
    def run(self, speed):
        return "%s runs %s" % (self.name, speed)

#Child class (inherits from Dog class)
class AustralianCattleDog(Dog):
    def run(self, speed):
        return "%s runs %s" % (self.name, speed)

#Create instances of dogs
my_dogs = [
    Labrador("Liza", 7)
    AustralianCattleDog("Peter", 13)
]

#Instantiate the Pets class
my_pets = Pets(my_dogs)

#Output
print("I    have    {    }    dogs."
.format(len(my_pets.dogs)))
for dog in my_pets.dogs:
    print("{ } is { }." .format(dog.name, dog.age))

print("They  are  all  classified  as  { }
.format(dog.species))
are_my_dogs_hungry = False
for dog in my_pets.dogs:
    if dog.is_hungry:
        are_my_dogs_hungry = True

if are_my_dogs_hungry:
    print("My dogs are hungry.")
else:
    print("My dogs are not hungry.")
```
(Real Python, 2018)

Conclusion

OOP is a programming paradigm that sets up structuring for your code. Objects, modules, inheritance, encapsulation, and polymorphism are just some of the key words to working with OOP. As it happens, OOP is also highly popular in other computing languages, so transferring your skills from Python's OOP to others is easy.

These concepts are essential to mastering OOP. The game we created with OOP in Python focused on constructing definitions to use later and concepts on which to easily fall back. By defining how the game is played within the system, launching the completed game is simple.

Chapter 6: Python Libraries and Frameworks

The basics are complete! You feel like a master programmer now, right? Well, there are several things to know yet. The first are the libraries and frameworks within Python.

Libraries and frameworks are designed to make programming easier. How? Information within libraries and frameworks are done by someone else. They are collections of information from outside sources that allow faster programming.

For example, suppose you wanted to create code for starting a game with interactions between a wizard and dragon, like that listed above. However, suppose the game becomes far more complex, introducing characters such as witches and knights that have impacts on game play. If you are not creating a game from scratch and would like to use information stored from an outside source, downloading the library and framework for this game may be the best option. After all, it takes time and effort to create large sequences of code, and it

95

may be easier to simply use a library from a

fellow coder.

Discovering new avenues of code is not necessarily the best option when time is of the essence or if you want to try out some code for fun. Since the Python community is growing every day, new libraries and frameworks are created for fun and to help other coders on their programming journeys.

What is a Library?

Libraries are the wide range of code in a programming language, and Python already comes with an extensive list. The syntax included in a library defines how information is created in the system. If you are curious about all of the information listed in the Python library, there are more than a few resources to provide that information.

There are a wide variety of libraries available to Python, and it is not uncommon to find a library used thousands, if not millions of times. These libraries provide modules that range from basic coding to advanced.

Popular Libraries and How to Install Them

If you do not have to create your own modules in Python, why start from the beginning? Some of the most popular Python libraries are available for free. Simple requests within Python can help you retrieve libraries. The "import" request brings all libraries into the system. Here are a few libraries that are available and how to install them.

Requests

Requests is available for free within the Python community. Requests has created a library that manipulates HTTP. Requests is mostly used for making queries in HTTP methods, customizing data including headers and footers, inspecting data from requests, and configuring data processing within the internet to improve the speed. The import function brings the library into Python, so we will start there.

Windows Install
Anaconda is a fantastic starting point for downloading libraries on Windows. Anaconda can be downloaded on their website www.anaconda.com/distributions. With Anaconda installed, the command to install requests is simple.

```
pip import requests
```

Linux Install
The Linux install for requests repeats that of Windows. If the command does not work, consider updating your software to the latest version. If you are using WindowsXP, some of the installing features may not work, so

installing pip manually is the only way to install requests.

```
pip install requests
```

Mac Install
Mac installation of requests follows the same lines as the others. The following command demonstrates a correct install.

```
pip install requests
```

Basics in Requests
The most basic modules inside requests are get( ) and post( ). Since Requests is designed to work in an internet setting, the get( ) query pulls in information from other URLs. It is often displayed as follows.

```
requests.get(thisisaurl.com)
        response
```

The response output brings shows the information from the website. The post( ) function acts as a portal to send information. It is displayed as follows.

```
requests.post(thisisaurl.com)
        response
```

The basic functions listed here are just the tip of the iceberg within the requests library. If you are interested in manipulating data within an internet setting and are serious about your future in coding, this is an essential library to obtain.

Scrapy

One of the most common web crawlers is Scrapy. A web crawler (also known as a web spider) browses the internet with complete automation. The extracted data from the searches within Scrapy keep websites up to date with current information, making a website better. Though it may seem illegal to mine for information, Scrapy offers a thoroughly legal way to get new information.

Windows Install

Installing Scrapy starts with downloading Anaconda. This system allows coders to simply import Scrapy from its database. The library connected with Scrapy comes with it. After installing Anaconda, open an Anaconda window to install Scrapy. Use the following code to install Scrapy.

```
conda install -c anaconda Scrapy
```

After this is complete, Scrapy is available for Python to use its library to create spiders on the world wide web.

Linux Install

Ubuntu 14.04 and above support Scrapy, but note that using the latest version will give you the best results. Versions of Ubuntu older than 14.04 may still work, but they will be considerably slower and may cause problems. Coding, however, becomes more complex than when installed through Windows. The code below is necessary to install Scrapy on Linux.

```
sudo apt-get install python-dev python-pip
libxml2-dev libxsltl-dev zliblg-dev libffi-dev
libssl-dev

sudo apt-get install python3 python3-dev
pip install scrapy (Python, n.d.)
```

Mac Install

Homebrew is necessary to install Scrapy, but, since it has already been installed, the code to install Scrapy is done through the steps below.

```
pip install scrapy
```

Numpy and Scipy

For those interested in mathematics and related fields, numpy is an absolutely essential library to add. Numpy's library contains many simple and complex mathematical terminology that is essential to using Python with regard to mathematics and similar fields. Scipy allows for graphical manipulations of data within the Python system. It provides operations to complete scientific calculations within Python.

Numpy, and its related cousin Scipy, hold libraries that define mathematical functions. Derivations, integrals, arrays, and plotting are only some of the features found in numpy. Scipy's library contains coding like other famous mathematical programs, such as MatLab. Though it may seem that numpy and Scipy are only useful to fields that constantly use mathematics, including these libraries to calculate basic functions within Python is absolutely essential.

Windows Install

With anaconda already installed on your computer, the route to installing numpy and Scipy libraries on any computer is relatively simple. Use the following code to install numpy and Scipy.

```
conda install -c anaconda numpy
conda install -c anaconda Scipy
```

Linux Install

Both Ubuntu and Debian support numpy and Scipy. Library managers usually install an older version of numpy and Scipy because they are more stable and popular. Follow the code below to install numpy and Scipy on Linux using apt-get.

```
sudo apt-get install python-numpy python-scipy
python-matplotlib ipython ipython-notebook
python-pandas python-sympy python-nose
(Python, n.d.)
```

Mac Install

Mac uses two different methods to install numpy and Scipy. Macports is common, but Macports is not automatically downloaded on every computer, so it requires both installs. Homebrew is also common, but it does not include the full ranges of both numpy and Scipy. Either is available for install with the code below.

For Macport

```
sudo port install py35-numpy py35-scipy py35-
matplotlib py35-ipython +notebook py35-pandas
py35-sympy py35-nose (Python, n.d.)
```

For Homebrew

```
brew install numpy scipy ipython jupyter
```

Pillow

For many interested in creating an artistic career within Python, Pillow offers programming that is unique in its ability to manipulate images. Also called PIL for Python Imaging Library, is designed to create modules that easily manipulate different types of images from JPEG to GIF to PDF. Pillow was created by Alex Clark and is available for free use, and the code is given by Python for Beginners.

Windows Install
Pillow is available for Windows users, however, only versions 2.6 and above can use the library due to more complex functions. Windows installs Pillow with the easy_install command as shown below.

```
easy_install pillow
```

Linux Install
Linux uses pip to install Pillow, and the same versions 2.6 and beyond apply to Linux devises. Linux installs Pillow with the sudo pip install command as shown below.

```
sudo pip install pillow
```

Mac Install

Pillow requires Homebrew to install Pillow. As Homebrew was already installed to install Python, there are no additional steps to download PIllow. When installing on a Mac, use the following two commands.

```
$ brew install libtiff libjpeg webp littlecms
$ sudo pip install pillow (Python, n.d.)
```

Though there are many other libraries that contain data more than helpful to coders, these libraries offer a good start.

How to Use a Library

The library within Python is highly extensive. If you recently downloaded Python and this is your first experience in creating code, you have already seen some modules in the software that are beneficial. The most recent version of Python will usually contain more modules than the others before it, so starting from scratch within Python is not the worst way to begin.

External libraries, however, are usually created by a single person or a few people who create libraries that suit various functions. For example, a library may contain data regarding mathematical equations while another simply focuses on their game's coding. Since there are many communities within the Python scope, coders have created numerous libraries to share with others. Different libraries have different named codes, so it is more than likely that these libraries will contain some of the same defined code. Python, however, creates the pathways to different modules, creating unique pathways for each module.

Functions within Libraries

Working through libraries is quite a feat, especially if you do not know everything they contain. However, some functions within Python allow for easy access to modules. Modules are like mini libraries; they break down all information in libraries into smaller, bite-sized pieces that are easier to manage. Building on modules can be done within Python and help to separate large groups of data to customize to a coder's specifications. Users can create modules by entering a bit of legitimate code and ending it with .py. The following functions already installed with the

Python system allow for easy access to modules.

The Dir( ) Function

The dir( ) function determines all definitions within a module and outputs the names in a list. When Python does not recognize new definitions, they are added one by one with each additional dir( ) function invoked (Sturtz, 2018). Namespaces, which are essentially lists that show an archive of names, display all defined names within the module.

Using a Module as a Script

Modules defined within Python are essentially scripts. When defining a code as a module, it is saved in Python's database. These are easily retrievable by entering that same module name listed before. Instead of listing the code contained in the module, it will deliver the output through a script.

What is a Framework?

One of the most loved parts of Python is its ability to handle frameworks. Frameworks make web applications easier to manage by keeping the necessary details to a minimum. Basically, frameworks keep coders from having to maintain "low-level details as protocols, sockets or process/thread management" (Python, n.d.). Coders using frameworks in Python must only focus on the logic of the code entered instead of breaking down all code to take each step piece by piece.

Frameworks are designed to process and interpret requests, produce responses, and store data. Frameworks that work together to create results for requests are called full-stack frameworks. Each framework acts as a step to the completed result, essentially making up a full stack.

Libraries and frameworks are essential to creating organized systems within Python. Since libraries already hold definitions and frameworks provide structure for web-based applications, they are the next step to creating a functional software.

Conclusion

Libraries and frameworks within Python are the bread and butter of the software. It is not necessary to create keywords by yourself, and it only makes sense to take advantage of the resources presented. Frameworks are the blueprints of the structures in Python. Their use is vital to keeping Python running.

You can easily install a library through the internet, and most of them are free. If you are thinking of creating libraries for others in the future, think of what information is the most valuable to the most people. Creating a list for one game and expecting to receive media coverage is impractical. Consider writing a library that will affect how people integrate with the system.

Make the most out of others' libraries by studying them and finding uses for the definitions. Though it is fun to create definitions from scratch, building your knowledge through following the examples of others is one of the best ways to improve. Have fun with the system and use the files as much as possible.

Chapter 7: Create Python Executable

If you go into file explorer located on every computer, a list of files are available for view for documents, pictures, and others. Executable files are those that end in .exe and are labeled as applications in file types. In this sense, Python is an executable. It is a program with software added to a computer, and it can behave independently. What if, however, you want to create something more with Python? Python can create games and applications, as demonstrated previously, and they can become applications.

Building an Executable File

The road to completing an executable file starts within Python, but, to be a decent application, it also should execute on desktops regardless of Python installation status. The first step to completing an executable is finding an application maker. The program we will install is cx_Freeze. Since you are already a pro at entering code, the step to download the file is simple.

python -m pip install cx_Freeze --upgrade

However, before downloading the software, take a look at what version of Pycharm you are using. If you are using a 32-bit version, the installation process will be slightly different than with a 64-bit version. If you need to find an alternative to the latest 64-bit version, others are available at https://sourceforge.net/projects/cx-freeze/files/. Remember to always choose the version that best applies to your computer.

Example: GoCart Racers

With cx_Freeze properly downloaded, import the library into Python. Since cx_Freeze works with Pygame, we want to extract the executable from the library.

```
import cx_Freeze

executables                              =
[cx_Freeze.Executable("pygameVideo15.py")]
```

The next step is to set up the game itself. As with all applications, modules, and variables in Python, the game must have a name. The other options for the setup must include the building blocks to the game, which means using a few packages from Pygame.

```
cx_Freeze.setup(
    name = "GoCart Racers"
    options  =   {"build_exe":   {"packages":
[pygame])}
    executables = executables
```

Since it is always better to be explicit than implicit, define where the information should go. Though Python is usually good at finding and placing files, it is always better to be safe than sorry. Define the path that the application must follow to create an executable.

```
C:/Pycharm/python setup.py build
```

When creating a game, the next step is to create options to pause the game or show "game over" for players. It is best to define text within the programming to make understanding the game easier. Following the example from Python Programming, we will create the executable within Python:

```
def paused( ):

        largeText                          =
pygame.font.SysFont(comicsansms", 115)
        TextSurf,          TextRect        =
text_objects("Paused", largeText)
        TestRect.center  =  ((display_width/2),
(display_height/2))
        gameDisplay.blit(TextSurf, TextRect)

        while pause:
            for event in pygame.event.get( ):

                if      event.type     ==
pygame.QUIT:
                    pygame.quit( )
                    quit( )

            #gameDisplay.fill(white)
            button("Continue, 150, 450, 100,
50, green, bright_green, unpause)
            button("Quit", 550, 450, 100, 50,
red, bright_red, quitgame)

            pygame.display.update( )
            clock.tick(15)          (Python
Programming, 2018)
```

This code creates conditions for the game. Both the "pause" and "game over" selections have been defined, which creates the basis for this game. Since the game is dependent on racing, it only makes sense to include the possibility of crashes. A crash in the game results in "game over," so, still following the example from Python Programming, we will enter the code as follows.

```
def crash( ):

    largeText                                =
pygame.font.SysFont("comicsansms", 115)
    TextSurf, TextRect = text_objects("You
Crashed", largeText)
    TextRect.center  =   ((display_width/2),
(display_height/2))
    gameDisplay.blit(TextSurf, TextRect)

    while True:
        for event in pygame.event.get( ):
            #print(event)
            if      event.type      ==
pygame.QUIT
                pygame.quit( )
                quit( )
        #gameDisplay.fill(white)

        button("Play Again", 150, 450,
100, 50, green, bright_green, game_loop)
        button("Quit", 550, 450, 100, 50,
red, bright_red, quitgame)

        pygame.display.update( )
        clock.tick(15)              (Python
Programming, n.d.)
```

With this code, the game_loop function should display as follows.

```
if x > display_width - car_width or x<0:
```

```
            crash( )
        if vehicle_starty > display_height:
            vehicle_starty = 0 - car_height
            vehicle_startx                  =
random.randrange(0, display_width)
            dodged += 1
            vehicle_speed  +=1
            vehicle_width += (dodged * 1.2)
        if y < vehicle_starty + vehicle_height:
            print("y crossover")

            if x > vehicle_startx and x <
vehicle_startx + vehicle_width or x+car_width
>   vehicle_startx  and  x  +  car_width  <
vehicle_startx = vehicle_width:
                print("x crossover")
                crash(       )         (Python
Programming, n.d.)
```

Those are the basics to create an executable within Python with regard to a racing game. The executable above is simply the start of getting a game running within Python, but it is just the tip of the iceberg. Creating a game that executes sounds and music in the background is yet another step in creating a game that will attract others. Games with these features are necessary to get ahead. But where to start? Well, Pygame has many features to help with game building, and adding music is one of the best. Pygame.mixer.Sound is a file within Pygame that offers a limited number of sounds for free. So, with that in mind, we will create a sound for a crash.

```
crash_sound = pygame.mixer.Sound("crash.wav")
```

Music can come from the Pygame library with pygame.mixer.music or from mp3 music right on your computer. The following code gives some examples of possible sounds in a game.

```
pygame.mixer.music.load("Track_1.mp3")
pygame.mixer.music.play(-1)
pygame.mixer.music.load("classical.wav)
pygame.mixer.music.play(-1)
```

The "-1" makes a song play indefinitely so the music will not stop until guided so with a code such as the following.

```
pygame.mixer.music.stop( )
```

Pretty simple, right? Simple musical code inputs add another level to an otherwise boring game, so play around with the sounds and music within Pygame when possible.

Exercise: Wizard's Game

With all of the information about how to create an executable with a gocart game, it is now time to move on to our own example: Wizard's Game. The code for setting up both the wizard and dragon has been completed. If you do not remember the game, here is a refresher.

A wizard and dragon do battle with each other. The wizard is attempting to destroy the dragon to inherit its castle. The dragon, misunderstood, has stored piles of gold within the castle and will not accept any other reward. Trying to save his hoard, the dragon fights back. Unbeknownst to the dragon, however, the wizard has potion to rejuvenate himself when the going gets rough. After he loses a "life," he can once again gain strength by injecting the potion directly into his arm. With renewed vigor, the wizard (that would be you) attacks the dragon again, hoping to steal the treasure and find the golden amulet within.

I know, that's a large premise for a simple executable example within Python, but it makes for a great story, doesn't it? The two objects within the program are the wizard and the dragon. Each have life points, mana points (which, to the uninitiated, are magical points), attack points, defense points, and defense points. The methods in Python show how each point is calculated. To begin the executable, let us start with the basics.

```
cx_Freeze.setup(
      name = "Wizard's Game"
      options  =   {"build_exe":   {"packages":
[pygame])}
      executables = executables
```

Once again, set up a place for the game to live to access it later. Define the pathway explicitly to find it easily in the future.

```
C:/Pycharm/python setup.py build/Wizard Game
```

Next, set up ways to both pause the game and create a "game over" result if the game is lost. Just like the example above, define the font, where the information will be displayed, and the consequences from actions within the game.

```
def paused( ):

        largeText                          =
pygame.font.SysFont(timesnewromanms", 100)
        TextSurf,              TextRect            =
text_objects("Paused", largeText)
        TestRect.center  =  ((display_width/2),
(display_height/2))
        gameDisplay.blit(TextSurf, TextRect)

        while pause:
                for event in pygame.event.get( ):

                if         event.type      ==
pygame.QUIT:
                        pygame.quit( )
                        quit( )

                #gameDisplay.fill(white)
                button("Continue,  500,  450,  100,
50,  green,  bright_green,  unpause)
                button("Quit",  500,  450,  100,  50,
red,  bright_red,  quitgame)

                pygame.display.update( )
                clock.tick(15)              (Python
Programming, n.d.)
```

Now it is time to define the rules of the game and how to execute them from within the game. Since the information within Python regarding the wizard and dragon have been stored, import those files to set up the executable, and let the games begin.

```
import time

import wizard
import dragon

response = str(input("Hello, what's your name ?\n"))
w1 = wizard.Wizard(response ,500, 500, 100, 100, 200,3)
d1 = dragon.Dragon(500, 200, 100, 100, 200)
endofWhile = False

w1.showStat()
# d1.showStat()
while endofWhile != True:
    ##Tower of the wizard
    goodResponse = False
    while goodResponse == False:
        response = str(input("What do you want to do "+ w1.name +"? \n 1 - Attack ; 2 - Take a potion ; 3 - Launch a fate \n"))
        if response != "1" and response != "2" and response != "3":
            print("Error, this is not a valid choice !!")
        else:
            goodResponse = True
            if response == "1":
                if d1.dragonChoice() == "1":
                    d1.life_pt = d1.life_pt - d1.dragonDefense(w1.atk_pt)
                    d1.showStat()
                elif d1.dragonChoice() == "2":
                    d1.life_pt = d1.life_pt - d1.dragonDodge(w1.atk_pt)
```

```python
                    d1.showStat()
                else:
                    d1.life_pt                      =
w1.wizardAttack(d1.life_pt)
                    print("Dragon              do
nothing...")
                    d1.showStat()
            elif response == "2":
                w1.takePotion()
                w1.showStat()
            else:
                w1.launchSpell()
                w1.showStat()


## Check if both opponents are still standing
    if d1.life_pt <= 0:
        endofWhile = True
        print("             xxxxxxxxxxxx\n")
        print("             You win \n")
        print("             xxxxxxxxxxxx\n")
        break
    elif w1.life_pt < 0 or w1.mana_pt < 0:
        endofWhile = True
        print("             xxxxxxxxxxxx\n")
        print("             You lose \n")
        print("             xxxxxxxxxxxx\n")
        break



    ##Tower of the dragon
    goodResponse = False
    while goodResponse == False:
        print("Dragon attack \n")
        response = str(input("What do you want
to do ? \n 1 - Defense; 2 - Dodge ; 3 - Take a
potion \n"))
        if response != "1" and response != "2"
and response != "3":
            print("Error, this is not a valid
choice !!")
        else:
            goodResponse = True
            if response == "1":
```

```
            w1.life_pt  =  w1.life_pt  -
w1.wizardDefense(d1.atk_pt)
            w1.showStat()
        elif response == "2":
            w1.life_pt  =  w1.life_pt  -
w1.wizardDefense(d1.atk_pt)
            w1.showStat()
        else:
            w1.takePotion()
            w1.life_pt
            w1.showStat()

    ## Check if both opponants are still
standing
    if d1.life_pt <= 0:
        endofWhile = True
        print("You win \n")
        break
    elif w1.life_pt < 0 or w1.mana_pt < 0:
        endofWhile = True
        print("              xxxxxxxxxxxx\n")
        print("              You lose \n")
        print("              xxxxxxxxxxxx\n")
        break
```

Create music files within the executable by using the pygame.mixer.music.load command, and discover what other sounds you can add to the game. Having epic music in the background is a great way for others to sink their teeth into your game.

Conclusion

We have discussed two examples within Python to create an executable. From creating a game to process racing in the GoCart Racing game to the Wizard, there are many ways to create games within Python. Games are not the only applications to create within Python, so there is a great opportunity to learn more about executables from visiting websites that define and walk you through the small steps. Python offers many opportunities to expand knowledge through communities, and Pycharm is a great place to start.

Chapter 8: Send Mail with SMTP

Have you ever wondered how you could send mail through your software program? Still, if you want to use your programming language for more than just creating executables and mathematics problems, Python is equipped with the ability to create and send mail through its programming.

Simple Mail Transfer Protocol (SMTP) creates a platform to transfer mail easily. System administrators, including those found online, use scripts to send emails from one person to another. It only makes sense that Python is able to do the same things. With the correct library, Python can create mail to send and create reminders for messages sent to you.

What is SMTP?

Python's SMTP library is accessed through smtplib, which is automatically downloaded with each current install. Python accesses the internet through any SMTP portal, supposing that it is set up to listen. Any provider can have an SMTP, and it is through communication between various ports that make sending mail possible. First, though, there is some terminology to discuss.

Host or Server

The host runs the SMTP server. The IP addresses and hostnames are all necessary to complete a transaction between sending host and receiver. Every host has its own URL that using SMTP that is specific to the host. For example, Google's mail server has a host URL of smtp.google.com. Each server responds as a beacon to other SMTP servers to collect mail and distribute it to the host which then translates the message and adds it to your inbox.

Mail sent from one server to another is done in code. As discussed earlier, computers use code in the form of binary numbers, and this is how mail is sent through servers. When the code reaches your inbox, instead of seeing a jumble of 0s and 1s, the receiving host translates the message to a readable form. This is why emails with larger content and attachments take longer to send.

Port

Most of sending mail occurs on the internet, but the only way to access the internet is through a port. A port is defined as a terminal with access to the internet where it is connected to the internet (TurboSMTP, n.d.). The most common port is 25, and post SMTP hosts use this, but it has its disadvantages. Spam and malware are easily transferred through port 25, so ports 465 or 587 are often used to avoid blockage from servers.

Local Hostname

For mail to know which mail is delivered where, each is defined by a hostname. Setting Python up with SMTP requires a local hostname, but that is not as difficult as it sounds. Computers are already set up with local hostnames which are found through a general search on your device. If you would like to change the name to one that is easier to remember or one you like better, each computer offers that service.

Protocol

A protocol within the Python universe describes a command. The idea behind SMTP is to develop protocols that will transfer data safely and reliably from one server to the next. Protocols are set up within every server to prevent inefficient transfers. Because protocols are already embedded into all servers, such as Google, Hotmail, AOL, or Yahoo!, data transfers become easier to track and prevent mistakes on a message's journey.

Learn to Send Mail

There are two ways to set up a mail service within Python. Many Python users choose to use an STMP service that has already been set up. Coders can use Google services to define elements within their own Python programming. The other option is to set up a local server, but that is not discussed here.

Using Google to Set up

Services like Gmail are helpful to set up an account, so we will discuss setting up a test account using Google. It is important to use a test account when using Google's SMTP because it will make serious changes to your account. Safety and security features need to be altered within a Gmail SMTP set up, which could make credential information easier to hack.

Set up a Gmail account by searching for google.com and using the top right corner to create an account. Once signed in, there are a few adjustments necessary to set up in Google's security and programming to make way for Python. Google works with Python versions 2.6 and later, so if you are working on a system that is out of date, now is the time to upgrade.

Enable API on Google by navigating to the API console within Google's service and selecting "Enable." Use the pip installer to install the Google Client library.

```
pip install --upgrade google-api-python-client
google-auth-httplib2 google-auth-oauthlib
```

Google then requests the following code in Python to test the connection:

```
from __future__ import print_function
import pickle
import os.path
from googleapiclient.discovery import build
from       google_auth_oauthlib.flow        import
InstalledAppFlow
from    google.auth.transport.requests    import
Request

# If modifying these scopes, delete the file
token.pickle.
SCOPES                                           =
['https://www.googleapis.com/auth/gmail.readon
ly']

def main():
    """Shows basic usage of the Gmail API.
    Lists the user's Gmail labels.
    """
    creds = None
    # The file token.pickle stores the user's
access and refresh tokens, and is
    #    created    automatically    when    the
authorization flow completes for the first
    # time.
    if os.path.exists('token.pickle'):
        with   open('token.pickle',   'rb')   as
token:
            creds = pickle.load(token)
    #  If  there  are  no  (valid)  credentials
available, let the user log in.
```

```python
    if not creds or not creds.valid:
        if creds and creds.expired and
creds.refresh_token:
            creds.refresh(Request())
        else:
            flow                        =
InstalledAppFlow.from_client_secrets_file(
                'credentials.json', SCOPES)
            creds                       =
flow.run_local_server(port=0)
        # Save the credentials for the next
run
        with open('token.pickle', 'wb') as
token:
            pickle.dump(creds, token)

    service      =     build('gmail',     'v1',
credentials=creds)

    # Call the Gmail API
    results                                  =
service.users().labels().list(userId='me').exe
cute()
    labels = results.get('labels', [])

    if not labels:
        print('No labels found.')
    else:
        print('Labels:')
        for label in labels:
            print(label['name'])

if __name__ == '__main__':
    main()  (Google, n.d.)
```

If it worked, Google will ask you to accept the programming, and you have officially set up Gmail with Python.

Send a Plain-Text Email

Since Gmail is already set up with a debugging server, there is no need to take additional steps to debug any incoming or outgoing mail. Creating a secure connection is the first step to sending an email, and SMTP_SSL( ) and .starttls( ) are the two codes necessary. SMTP_SSL( ) is set up for a secure SMTP connection, and .starttls( ) provides an encrypted version of the email to an unsecure SMTP connection. Python suggests using ssl model of TLS, which is a secure encrypter.

SMTP_SSL( )

The code below is used for setting up a secure email with a TLS-encrypted message that Google provides. The downloaded Google Client library has this definition, so there is no need for clarification.

```python
import smtplib, ssl

port = 465  # For SSL
password = input("Password")

context = ssl.create_default_context( )

with smtplib.SMTP_SSL("smtp.gmail.com", port,
context=context) as server:
```

```
server.login("yourgmailnamehere@gmail.com",
password) (Google, n.d.)
```

Creating a place for a password within the code is neither practical nor safe. Instead, use the input( ) command to find the password and use the .getpass( ) command in the Google Client library displays the password if you forget it (Langen, 2018). Otherwise, keep a copy of your password handy for the future.

Sending the email through SMTP_SSL( ) is then set up as any email account may send using this code.

```
sender_email = "mygmailaccount@gmail.com"
receiver_email = "yourgmailaccount@gmail.com"
message = """\
Subject: Any Subject

Any message"""
#Send email
```

.starttls( )
Because requirements for .starttls( ) are not set up with an encrypted service, the .starttls( ) command encrypts the information within an SMTP connection. Setup for .starttls( ) is relatively easy and is given by the following command.

```
import smtplib, ssl

smtp_server = "smtp.gmail.com"
port = 587
```

```
sender_email = "youremailaddress@gmail.com"
password = input("Password")

context = ssl.create_default_context( )
try:
    server = smtplib.SMTP(smtp_server,port)
    server.ehlo() # Can be omitted
    server.starttls(context=context)
    server.ehlo( )
    server.login(sender_email, password)
    # TODO: Send email here
except Exception as e:
    # Print any error messages to stdout
    print(e)
finally:
    server.quit( )
```

This function is completed in a try window, which allows testing but does not commit to the programming until it is removed. To send mail, use the .starttls( ) or .sendmail( ) commands.

Sending an email through .starttls( ) is more complicated than it is in SMTP_SSL( ) because the email requires encrypting. The code for sending this type of email is given by the following.

```
import smtplib, ssl

port = 465
smtp_server = "smtp.gmail.com"
sender_email = "mygmailaddress@gmail.com"
receiver_email = "yourgmailaddress@gmail.com"
password = input("Password")
message = """\
Subject: Any Subject

Any message. """
```

```
context = ssl.create_default_context( )
with     smtplib.SMTP_SSL(smtp_server,     port,
context = context) as server:
     server.login(sender_email, password)
     server.sendmail(sender_email,
receiver_email, message) (Langen, 2018)
```

Though the process is more complicated, it is best-practice to use this style on servers you do not trust.

HTML Emails

Sending plain text emails is fun and everything, but what about more complex emails? Links included in emails are slightly more complicated than their plain text counterparts, but they are still possible within Python.

For security reasons, some choose not to open outside links, so it is safer to send them in plain text. However, Python's Multipurpose Internet Mail Extensions (MIME) sends emails in both plain text and HTML. The email.mime library has multiple modules to make the transition easier. Below, Joska de Langen (2018) gives an example code through Real Python to exhibit how the email is sent.

```
import smtplib, ssl
```

```python
from email.mime.text import MIMEText
from email.mime.multipart import MIMEMultipart

sender_email = "my@gmail.com"
receiver_email = "your@gmail.com"
password = input("Type your password and press
enter:")

message = MIMEMultipart("alternative")
message["Subject"] = "multipart test"
message["From"] = sender_email
message["To"] = receiver_email

# Create the plain-text and HTML version of
your message
text = """\
Hi,
How are you?
Real Python has many great tutorials:
www.realpython.com"""
html = """\
<html>
  <body>
    <p>Hi,<br>
       How are you?<br>
       <a
href="http://www.realpython.com">Real
Python</a>
       has many great tutorials.
    </p>
  </body>
</html>
"""

# Turn these into plain/html MIMEText objects
part1 = MIMEText(text, "plain")
part2 = MIMEText(html, "html")

# Add HTML/plain-text parts to MIMEMultipart
message
# The email client will try to render the last
part first
message.attach(part1)
message.attach(part2)
```

```
# Create secure connection with server and
send email
context = ssl.create_default_context()
with   smtplib.SMTP_SSL("smtp.gmail.com",   465,
context=context) as server:
    server.login(sender_email, password)
    server.sendmail(
        sender_email,           receiver_email,
message.as_string()
    ) (Langen, 2018)
```

As you can see, sending code with HTML code is far more complex. Ports, libraries, and HTML links and plain text must be included to complete the transaction. Just as with plain text emails, a secure connection is essential to sending an email. Without secure connections, the HTML link may lead to malware incursion. Sending plain text with the HTML link is both safer and more convenient.

Conclusion

Sending emails through Python may look complicated, but choosing the right tools and libraries make transitioning to emails through coding much easier. It is important to know the hosts, ports, and local hostnames of both the device on which you are working and others.

Using Python to create emails usually includes setting up shop with a large SMTP server, in this case, Google. Using this method is easier on coders and creates libraries for SMTP users, eliminating the agonizing path through completing a new library. `SMTP_SSL( )` and `.starttlc( )` are the two methods that transfer files to other servers. While `SMTP_SSL( )` is the easier of the two, it also requires more security. In short, whichever function you decide to use, remember to pay attention to the syntax and make sure all pathways are secure.

Chapter 9: Databases

Databases are the bread and butter of programming. Why? Databases hold all the data that is entered within the system. Databases hold libraries, sequences, and, perhaps most importantly, sequences for ordering data within the system. Imagine using a large moving truck when moving to another city. Inside the moving truck there may be blankets, pillows, dishes, clothes, paintings, vacuums, a tv, movies, and a bed. Now imagine that boxes did not exist, and everything you own had to fit within the truck by itself.

If you are a good packer, you may organize the items into suitable piles that fit relatively well together. However, when the moving truck starts driving to the destination, all items within the truck will bounce about and leave nothing of organization left. Assuming you are a terrible packer, the items would be strewn about with no noticeable organization. Either way, the "stuff" within the moving truck will be spread out in pieces, maybe with some objects torn or broken.

Now let us relieve some of that stress by now accepting that boxes exist and separators within the truck are available. The organization of the materials will not only be much better, but they will also keep everything in place. If the organization within the moving truck is perfect, no items within the truck will budge, and the neat fairies express their love for your work. Databases offer the same organization for the data entered. All the modules, definitions, and functions we have talked about now become established within the "moving truck" of programming systems.

What is a Database?

Like we have already discussed, a database is an established frame within a software that organizes all data and data types. However, there is more than one type of database, but we will only focus on three: hierarchical, networked, and relational. Each of these databases not only organizes information in different ways, but they retrieve data differently as well.

Hierarchical Database

A hierarchical database may be best illustrated with royalty. We are not saying that the database in and of itself is only useful to aristocracy, but it does help clarify the point. Imagine a kingdom with a ruling king and queen. They have three children who each marry and have three children. So far, the king and queen have nine grandchildren. Now imagine a department store that has four classes of clothing: women, men, girls, and boys. Each of these classifications have products in shoes, shirts, pants, belts, bedding, and crafting. Each of these classifications have their own subcategories.

Hierarchical databases are handy for small jobs, but when the subcategories become so large that it becomes unwieldy, they become less helpful. Databases that have this structure cannot handle large amounts of data. When the list of subcategories becomes enormous, programs must wade through links and connections until they get to the correct response. As you can imagine, it takes some time to process information if the hierarchical chain becomes too long. It is comparable to wading through paper to find the right subcategory only to find that other subcategories hold the answers.

Networking Database

A networking database has links to other sections and subcategories within the database. For example, think of social media. Suppose you are trying to find someone from highschool that you found out was arrested for kitten-napping. Obviously, this thief was not in your group of friends from school, so they are not connected to you through social media.

However, you sister has a friend who has a brother who has a cousin who has a grandfather who has an acquaintance who knows this robbing fiend. If you have enough energy to wade through the sentence, you eventually find the person you have been looking for.

Networking databases are similar to this. Imagine entering data for the animals in a partnered zoo and you really want to adopt their rhino. With that simple connection, it is easy to find information within the database to retrieve information. However, assuming that you have a large list of zoos in your database, there may be a unique spotted monkey that catches your attention. To find the characteristics of that monkey, you must find the link between your zoo and your partner's zoo, then the link your partner has with San Diego, then the link the San Diego Zoo has with an Ecuadorian zoo, and it is only through this exotic zoo that has the rights to request information from an Argentinian zoo who happens to have the monkey. The list of zoos available in your database would have to be astronomical to create all those links. In order to find the Argentinian zoo, you must wade through links and partnerships, which takes precious time and patience. Networking databases are also not ideal for large quantities of data.

Relational Database

The final database for discussion is the relational database. What is better to hold data than a table? Tables are useful because of their easy access and finding information within them is much easier. Relational databases are unique because they can break data down into pieces that are independent to an object or tables that hold whole inventories.

Imagine a humane society taking care of animals that needs to keep both their dogs and their sister kennel's dogs within the same system. A relational database can keep all information within both systems on a single table. If we are not careful, the relational database can end up like the others (full of data but with a massive processing time). Relational databases, however, can break down tables from the very largest to the smallest. The columns of every table decide the categories of all types table. The rows are inputted data for the information that matches those columns.

For example, within the large database for the humane society and its sister kennel, the humane society and its sister kennel want to have a record of all dogs at both locations. The only information they need displayed within that table is the name, ID number, and breed of each dog. Because there is no limit to the number of rows allowed on a table, the kennels can add as many dogs as they would like. Breaking the table down gives more information for both kennels and for each dog. One of the smallest tables may include data exclusively for a dog named Max. The table may include columns for records of feeding times, exercise per day, and how many times he has been visited.

MySQL and Creating an SQL Table

MySQL is a database in which data can be created, stored, and modified. It is available for free at https://www.mysql.com/downloads/, and creating code in Python makes for an easy transition into learning databases. The first step to importing all libraries into Python is using the familiar import command. The next is to set up a connecter access all data.

```
import mysql.connector
mydb = mysql.connector.connect(
    host = "Your local machine here"
    user = "Username"
    password = "Password"
)

print(mydb)
```

Creating a database includes creating a cursor, and its command is also simple.

```
mycursor = mydb.cursor( )
mycursor.execute         =("CREATE       DATABASE
mydatabase)
```

So, how do you create a table in Python using MySQL? Table creation is just as simple as the code above.

```
mycursor = mydb.cursor( )
mycursor.execute = ("CREATE TABLE Dog Kennels
name(VARCHAR  (200))  ID_number(VARCHAR  (200))
breed(VARCHAR (200)))
```

Insert Data

Inserting data into a database is essential to creating effective tables, and it is the first step to creating a basis within the software. The INSERT INTO( ) command defines both the table and column in which data is inserted. The command also determines in which column the information will land. Data inserted into the table displays as rows on the table. Columns are formed with a table, as we have seen above, so the only data needed are the values associated with the columns. The VALUES( ) command displays all data entered into the table separated by a column.

Let us break down this information with an example. A library enters the information for books into a database. Five new books were recently purchased and placed into three different categories: horror, fiction, and biography. The table, therefore must include the name of the book, the author, and the category for which each applies. The code for inserting data into this table is displayed as follows.

```
INSERT INTO books(Title, Author, Genre)
VALUES("Carrie", "Stephen King", "Horror")
        ("Things Fall Apart", "Chinua Achebe",
"Fiction")
        ("The Haunting of Hill House", "Shirley
Jackson", "Horror")
        ("Harry Potter and the Deathly Hallows",
"J.K. Rowling", "Fiction")
        ("Alexander Hamilton", "Ron Chernow",
"Biography")
```

The table then includes all titles listed here. Additional entries displaying more specific results may be broken down into additional tables.

Select Data

Selecting data within a database is essential to its development. Without knowing what is in a database, it is difficult to make changes and decisions about programming. Fortunately, Python offers the fetchone( ) and fetchall( ). Data stored within a database is accessed through these functions provide one or all of a column or table. Multiple columns and tables may be selected to display information.

For example, if the library is curious about all the books in the fiction section, the code would define a column. The code would read as follows.

```
try:
    dbconfig = red_db_config( )
    conn = MySQLConnection(**dbconfig)
    cursor.execute("SELECT * FROM books")

    row = cursor.fetchone( )

    while row is not None:
        print(row)
        row = cursor.fetchone( )
```

This simple code defines all books within that column. Now, if the entire table of books is necessary for inventory, the code may read like the following.

```
try:
    dbconfig = read_db_config( )
    conn = MySQLConnection(**dbconfig)
    cursor = conn.cursor( )
    cursor.execute("SELECT * FROM books")
    rows = cursor.fetchall( )

    print("Total Row(s):", cursor.rowcount)
    for row in rows:
        print(row)
```

The asterisk attached to each of these commands indicates "all."

Update Data

Occasionally it is necessary to update data within the system. When creating a foundation with customers, it is customary to have their address, phone numbers, names, and orders. People are known to move, change phone numbers, update names, and buy more orders, which makes keeping static tables in Python impractical. Fetching data is the first step to changing information within the database, but

MySQL's update( ) query. The example below is retrieved through MySQL's own site.

```
try:
        connection                                    =
mysql.connector.connect(host = "localhost",

        database = "electronics")
        cursor = connection.cursor( )
        sql_update_query = """Update laptop set
price = %s where id = %s"""
        inputData = (price, id)
        cursor.execute(sql_update_query,
inputData)
        connection.commit( )
```

Delete Data

Sometimes it is also necessary to delete data within a database. Even though relational databases are far superior in their capacities to hold data than hierarchical or networking databases, they can still become gummed up when years of data enters the system. Deleting data is one of the most important functions within MySQL to keep processing moving smoothly.

For example, consider a used car dealership. There are many aspects of the business, but some of the most difficult things to keep track of are contracts. Whether they are utilizing cash, outside finance, in-house finance, or wholesales, keeping track of all information within the system becomes tricky. With over 100 car sales each month, the number of accounts within the database can reach beyond 12,000 over a ten year period. With all that data within the system, deleting the old accounts is the best option to keep the database running smoothly.

Deleting data may also be necessary to protect identities from theft. Using the used car business example, there may be thousands of social security numbers, phone numbers, dates of birth, and addresses that are private information. Deleting data from the database keeps customers safe and improves loyalty if they know that their information is in good hands.

Delete data from inside the system requires the delete( ) query. Pynative displays an example that we will discuss here.

```
try:
        cursor = connection.cursor ( )
        sql_Delete_query = """Delete from Laptop
where id = %s"""
        laptopID = 2
        cursor.execute(sql_Delete_query,
(laptopID,))
        connection.commit ( )
        print("Record Deleted successfully")
```

```
except mysql.connector.Error as error:
    print("Failed to Delete record from
table:{}".format(error))
finally:
    if (connection.is_connected( )):
        cursor.close( )
        print("MySQL    connection    is
closed")
```

Conclusion

Databases are some of the most important parts of creating within Python. Relational databases are those that define tables and send data into those tables. It is through this type of database that information can be stored securely. Tables created provide locations for information to stay, and they ultimately keep information sorted into useful groups. Use MySQL as a free resource and database to continue to add data.

Inserting, selecting, updating, and deleting data are the four vital queries to starting keep a database current. Data manipulation allows processors to complete commands in an SQL database called queries. Any information, be it rows, columns, or whole tables, are manipulated by these four processes.

Chapter 10: Concurrent and Parallel Programming

Wouldn't it be nice if there were a way to use two Python commands at the same time? Luckily, Python is set up for this property, and it is rapidly becoming a necessary way to use operations in the software. Concurrent and parallel programming are the two ways to achieve this.

Contrary to popular belief, concurrent and parallel programming are not the same things. Each work on the basis of operating two threads at the same time, but the way they process is slightly different. Concurrent processes *appear* to work at the same time, and each window will show its status. Parallel programming occurs when both processes are *actually* working at the same time.

Concurrent and parallel programming are dependent on threading. A thread is a file process execution. So, multiple threads working at the same time can become difficult to maintain if they each require a lot of CPU.

Concurrent and parallel programming each have their own benefits and drawbacks.

Concurrent threads work one at a time, but they show as two processed developments working at the same time. This can either speed up or slow down coding significantly. If one process is running a heavy program, it is unlikely that the second process will work as quickly. Think about messaging two friends at once. If you work concurrently when sending a message back, one friend will receive the message first, and the second friend will follow after that. With short messages, this works relatively quickly. However, if the first friend has sent a long text explaining a dire situation and want thorough feedback, it will take some time to get back to the second friend. To your friends, it will appear as you are working on sending replies to both of them at the same time.

Parallel threads work together. Parallel threads can also work either quickly or slowly, depending on the circumstances. Large projects processing at the same time can really slow down production if one of the threads requires a long processing time. However, short and simple threads can work quickly, and both will finish at the same time. Let us go back to the messaging example. Your two friends are expecting messages at the same time. If your returning messages are simple, like "I'll be right there," the time to process them will be simple. However, consider both texts sent are radically different in size. Friend one still wants advice about how to handle a new boy's attention, and friend two simply wants to know when you will be at the party. Since you are working in parallel, both texts must be sent at the same time. That means you have to break up the work between the two. Friend one may get a few words, and friend two may get a single letter. The best reason to use parallel programming is when one process depends on outside inputs.

With concurrent and parallel programming, it becomes essential to separate the functions into easy-to-access sections. Various tools from within Python prevent change from too many files. Others require specific access to change data within the system. The SQL relational database is set up with three types of locks to prevent overprocessing in Python.

When there are multiple people work within a database, information can change quickly. If an entire company uses the same database, and two or more people try to change the same information at the same time, results could be hazardous. Assume that one of these people is in the sales department and wants to edit the information of a particular client. Someone else in the customer service field also has access to that customer and wants to change the billing information and address within the system. If the customer service representative changes the information in the system before the sales person has a chance to change anything, and incorrect information may be saved.

Consider a more pressing situation. Suppose an accountant tracking inventory and money made in a system works with another accountant who has access to the system as well. Unbeknownst to the first accountant, the second accountant adds transactions and changes dates on others. Without locks on the system and both attempting to make changes, the information may save twice, throwing the books completely out of whack. Locks, mutual exclusions, and deadlocks prevent issues with multiple access.

Locks

One of the most important features in concurrent and parallel programming is the lock. From the example above, it is very clear that completing transactions (which is what we call processes in the SQL world) with multiple people accessing the same information at the same time causes chaos. Locks in SQL determine the condition of the database when it is accessed from multiple locations. Locks are available on multiple levels, and this exclusivity is necessary for multiple practices. The levels range from overall locking, which locks the entire database, to simple data locking, which only locks small transactions during processes.

Though locking the entire database seems a tad extreme, it has its benefits. For example, consider a database that is shared through a server. If the software is contained on the one server, updating the system requires that all external points must be shut down. Updating is one of the main reasons to lock an entire database, and it is the most common. Therefore, most developed software contains an option for locking the whole database. On the flip side, if an incorrect locking mechanism is added to the system, processes on other computers slow down considerably. Take caution when developing a lock that shuts down all transactions.

Locking on the smallest level takes slices of information from tables and places locks only when accessed by an individual. This is one of the most common locks within the SQL system. Locking data in the software through mutual exclusion can refer to one data point, but we will get into that later.

Table locking is another common method of locking. Because SQL is based on the use of relational tables, separating tables into smaller chunks is the best option within SQL. If the database only consists of one table, table locking would lock the entire database, which would slow down processes considerably. However, breaking down tables into parent / child tables (which consist of a master list and its offspring, which may be a specialized subsection of the main table's theme) makes locking tables more valuable. In large businesses, it is best to unlock the table as quickly as possible.

Mutual Exclusion

Mutual exclusions play the first-come-first-serve game. The first person to access an area of the database has an exclusive lock on the changes within the software. This means that, whatever changes they make, they are given sole priority. No other members of the business can create a lock when a mutual exclusion lock is in play. Two transactions can occur at the same time, but the mutual exclusion lock takes precedence.

So what does that really mean? Imagine you are part of a university and you want to make some changes on the software. The student's address and GPA changed after the end of the semester. Another executive assistant also has access to the student's records, and he or she wants to change the billing address in the Python table. Are they both able to change the information in the system? Yes. Though they are accessing the same student, both of them are accessing different information from the student's page. They can each complete their transactions and close the table, removing any exclusive locks on the data.

Now consider the example but both executive assistants try to access the billing address at the same time. The first executive assistant accesses the billing address first, so he or she has an exclusive lock on the billing address. Can both both executive assistants change the billing address at the same time? No. Each person works within a mutual exclusion locking system, which means the first person to complete the transaction takes precedence.

The code within Python to lock and unlock sections with mutual exclusions are given through the mutex.lock( ) and mutex.unlock( ) commands. The mutex.lock( ) command requires the function and argument to complete a transaction.

```
mutex.lock(function, argument)
```

```
mutex.unlock( )
```

The queries are remarkably simple, and they make processing information through concurrent and parallel programming easier. These locks prevent parallel programming to gum up on simpler tasks.

Deadlocks

Deadlocks are the most common problems when running SQL. As we have discussed previously, it is possible for two people to access the same information at the same time, but locks stacking on top of each other can cause problems. If a lock becomes "stuck," no one else can access the information, which leads to errors. In a large business, this can become detrimental to business.

Deadlocks occur when two or more users flip locks. For example, if person A is accessing John Doe's table to find data relating to his customer purchases and person B is looking at John Doe's repayment record, both have exclusive access to those areas with an exclusive lock. However, if person A tries to access John Doe's repayment record at the same time that person B access his repayment record and vice versa, a deadlock occurs. Each lock is attempting to lock for the new user. Sometimes these deadlocks appear as slow processing, and others appear to completely stop functionality within the software. Either way, it is essential to debug deadlocks.

Creating a debugging code is different since there are multiple reasons why a deadlock occurs. When you go further into development, the easier it is to identify the problem. For now, however, prevent multiple locks by creating mutual exclusion locks. Because they can work within small sections, they are the best bet to prevent deadlocks.

Race Conditions

What happens when multiple processes try to retrieve the same information at the same time? Well, if you are in a sack race and all trying to get to the finish line (which happens to be a slot two feet wide), there will be mayhem. Now, imagine everyone is evenly matched, jump at the same time, land the same distance apart, and reach the slot at the same time. Whacked heads and limbs flying in a flurry of burlap will prevent everyone from crossing the finish line.

Race conditions occur when more than one process tries to run at the same time. When two threads are submitted in quick succession, instead of processing them together, Python must process them one at a time for successful conclusion. This usually means that one process is dependent on another to finish. The increment( ) command helps to move the process along faster. Example code is written below:

```
lock.aquire( )
increment( )
lock.release( )
```

This code creates faster running time within the software, and though it may seem like mere milliseconds are shaved off the processing time, when larger queries are used, it could shave off minutes. It is well worth the time.

Conclusion

Using SQL is a great way to create a database using Python. It is important, though, to keep in mind which processes you are using to complete transactions. Concurrent programming processes appear to work at the same time, but they actually work one at a time. This is one of the most common processes in programming, and it may shave off more time than parallel programming. Parallel programming completes two transactions at the same time. If they are both simple, parallel programming is easy and efficient. However, it takes more time with large threads, making it less efficient than concurrent programming.

Locks are essential to maintaining a database. They can be created to lock small sections, like single data, or large sections, like shutting down all processes to update the system. Mutual exclusions prevent deadlocks because they provide broken-down data chunks to prevent locks becoming jumbled. Race conditions determine how fast a transaction will complete, and using increments, processing speeds can decrease significantly.

Chapter 11: Socket

Since it is abundantly clear that programming involves a wide variety of attachments to complete transactions and make processing simpler, the next step is to move onto sockets. Sockets send messages across networks (Nathan Jennings, 2018). Networks can be local (like the network on your computer that allows you to see information from another station) or external (the internet is a great example).

With the introduction of the world wide web, networking became essential and more than a little popular. Application Programming Interfaces (API) became wildly popular, and many of the basic functions of APIs are in use today. The most common interfacing methods is through server-client interactions. What does this mean? A server has all information within its database and the client interacts with the server, providing updates and sending them back to the server.

Socket APIs carry modules that essential to connection with other networks. The most basic of these are listed below from Real Python's Nathan Jennings.

- ☒ `socket()`
- ☒ `bind()`
- ☒ `listen()`
- ☒ `accept()`
- ☒ `connect()`
- ☒ `connect_ex()`
- ☒ `send()`
- ☒ `recv()`
- ☒ `close()`

As we have touched on in the past, Python has an extensive library of its own, so these functions are already included in its vast resources.

Transition Control Protocols (TCP) are responsible for sending the information securely across a network. In the section discussing sending mail, we showed that TCP made communications with the internet more reliable, sending mail that is made to display in order. This is essential to constructing sockets with Python. Assuming a connection is lost when trying to process a transaction, TCP determines the success of the sent data and resends it if processing failed.

TCPs have "handshakes" that connects a server

to client. Imagine these handshakes as pathways to information. The server listens to data sent to it using the codes listed below:

- `socket( )`

- `bind( )`
- `listen( )`
- `accept( )`

The TCP then hands this information over to the client. The client, in turn, sends a `socket( )` response, which allows access to the server. Both client and server then communicate with each other through `send( )` and `recv( )` commands, providing a pathway to each other. Once the transactions are complete, the client then sends the `close( )` command, which disconnects the link between the two.

Echo Client and Server

Knowing the connection between server and client, we can now set up a method by which the server will echo what the client sends. Once this is complete, we will review the opposite: the client will echo what the server sends. This proves communication between server and client for further communications. Because networking between server and client is difficult, do not be afraid to break this section down for better understanding.

Echo Server

Real Python's Nathan Jennings (2018) provides excellent examples of code. The code has been modified to understand the communication between a server and client on the same internet socket. The IP address from the host is connected to a local router, and the client's received information comes from port 425.

```
import socket

HOST = "192.168.2.25"       #Standard   loopback
interface address for a local host
PORT = 2425                 #Port  listening  to
the server

with              socket.socket(socket.AF_INET,
socket.SOCK_STREAM) as s:
        s.bind((HOST, PORT))
        s.listen( )
        conn, addr = s.accept( )
        with conn:
                print("Connected", addr)
                while True:
                        data = conn.recv(5235)
                        if not data:
                                break
                        conn.sendall(data)
```
(Jennings, 2018)

Data is instructed to be sent through the client to the server. The host requires an IP address like 127.1.25.2 to create a loopback interface which keeps data moving `smootly`. `socket.socket( )` displays which devices should share a connection and identifies the sockets through which information passes. The two sockets listed within the code refer to the internet (`AF_INET`) and TCP (`SOCK_STREAM`) to send a secure and reliable code from the client to the server. `AF_INET` refers to IPv4, which is displayed in the host name. s.bind connects the two sockets `together`. `listen( )` and `accept()` provides an open path for communication.

Now to the second half of this code. The `conn.recv( )` command receives the information and is ordered to send the data back. The while loop creates an endless stream of information back and forth.

Echo Client

The code for receiving an echo on the client from the server is remarkably easier and is given by the following code:

```
import socket

HOST = 192.168.3.10 #Server's host name or IP
address
PORT = 3465         #Port used by the server

with                socket.socket(socket.AF_INET,
socket.SOCK_STREAM) as s:
       s.connect((HOST, PORT))
       s.sendall(b "Random text")
       data = s.recv(3465)
print("Received", repr(data)) (Jennings, 2018)
```

And there it is! It follows the same outline as
the other, but TCP is not necessary to send the
information with this method.

Multi-Connection Client and Server

Connections between clients and servers
become more useful when there are more of
them. Think about it: receiving information
into your database is beneficial, but if you
receive a large chunk of data from several
different processors, using only one connection
can delay precious time. If you want to become
a rockstar in the programming field, shaving
off as much time as possible is one of the best
goals to make.

Multiple connections between clients and servers can become tricky, however. Multiple applications and modules are available for download to help with the process of handling tons of information flooding into your database. The one we will discuss is called Asynchronous I/O, and it is already available on the latest version of Python. `asynchio` creates a platform for working with multiple tasks, and it is one of the most beneficial tools in Python.

Multi-Connection Server

To set up multiple connects, we must first break it down into servers and clients. Below is another code from Nathan Jennings. The code is used for a multi-connection server. Once again, we will break it down so everything makes sense. The first step is to set up a listening socket.

```
import selectors
sel = selectors.DefaultSelector( )

lsock      =      socket.socket(socket.AF_INET,
socket.SOCK_STREAM)
lsock.bind((host, port))
lsock.listen( )
print("listening on", (host,port))
lsock.setblocking(False)
```

```
sel.register(lsock, selectors.EVENT_READ, data
= None)
```
(Jennings, 2018)

Most of this should look familiar. The code for setting up a socket requires identification of the sockets, binding the connections, and setting up the feed to listen. The new elements are `lsock.setblockting(False)` which prevents socket blocking. `sel.select( )` and `sel.register( )` select the information and register the socket for monitoring respectively (Jennings, 2018). Next we will define the event loop and `accept_wrapper( )` function.

```
def accept_wrapper(sock):
        conn, addr = sock.accept( )
        print("accepted connection from", addr)
        conn.setblocking(False)
        data   =   types.SimpleNamespace(addr   =
addr, inb = b " ", outb = " ")
        events      =      selectors.EVENT_READ      |
selectors.EVENT_WRITE
        sel.register(conn, events, data = data)
```
(Jennings, 2018)

The sockets set up this code need blocking to prevent other sockets from accessing the information during the transition. sel.select(timeout = None) keeps the line open for communication. The accept_wrapper( ) function is the next step to setting up the server, and it is defined with the code listed below.

173

```
def service_connection(key, mask):
    sock = key.fileobj
    data = key.data
    if mask & selectors.EVENT_READ:
        recv_data = sock.recv(1024)
        if recv_data:
            data.outb += recv_data
        else:
            print("closing connection
to", data.addr)
            sel.unregister(sock)
            sock.close()
    if mask & selectors.EVENT_WRITE:
        if data.outb:
            print("echoing",
repr(data.outb), "to", data.addr)
            sent                      =
sock.send(data.outb)
            data.outb                 =
data.outb[sent:]  (Jennings, 2018)
```

The functions `selectors.EVENT_READ`, `sock.accept( )`, and `conn.setblocking(False)` set up the event to read, allows the socket to transfer data, and sets up blocking respectively. All are necessary to complete a successful transaction. The server is set up to block all other connections, but not those listening from the socket we are trying to use. Finally, we define the event and client to accept the information.

Multi-Connection Client

Because a client receives information from the server, its process is slightly different. The main function for completing a multi-connection with the client is through the start_connections ( ) : command. First it must be defined before we can dig deeper into the coding.

```
def start_connections(host, port, num_conns):
    sever_addr = (host, port)
    for i in range(0, num_conns):
        connid = i + 1
        print("starting        connection",
connid, "to", server_addr)
        sock                              =
socket.socket(socket.AF_INET,
socket.SOCK_STREAM)
        sock.setblocking(False)
        sock.connect_ex(server_addr)
        events = selectors.EVENT_READ |
selectors.EVENT_WRITE
        data                              =
types.SimpleNamesspace(connid = connid,

    msg_total = sum(len(m) for m in
                                       m
                                       e
                                       s
                                       s
                                       a
                                       g
                                       e
                                       s
                                       )

    recv_total = 0
```

```
            messages = list(messages),

            outb = b " ")
                    sel.register(sock, events, data =
data) (Jennings, 2018)
```

The `num_conns` command, as you might expect, tells the client how many connections it is to make without blocking the connections. Perhaps one of the biggest differences in this code compared with the server's code is the `connect_ex( )` command, which sends an error message if no connection is made. Just as was learned early in this book, classification is necessary for the creation of full functions. Since the client is receiving data from the server, its class is defined as types.SimpleNamespace. The next step is to look at the `service_connection( )` command, like our example with the server.

```
def service_connection(key, mask):
        sock = key.fileobj
        data = key.data
        if mask & selectors.EVENT_READ:
                recv_data = sock.recv(1024)
                if recv_data:
                        print("received",
repr(recv_data),        "from        connection",
data.connid)
                        data.recv_total        +=
len(recv_data)
                if        not        recv_data        or
data.recv_total == data.msg_total:
                        print("closing
connection", data.connid)
```

```
                sel.unregister(sock)
                sock.close( )
        if mask & selectors.EVENT_WRITE:
            if      not       data.outb      and
data.messages:
                data.outb                    =
data.messages.pop(0)
            if data.outb:
                print("sending",
repr(data.outb). "to connection", data.connid)
                sent                         =
sock.send(data.outb)
                data.outb                    =
data.outb[sent:] (Jennings, 2018).
```

And that is it! Completing these two codes
creates an environment that is easily controlled
by using their definitions.

Multi-Connection Client and Server

It is important to save each of these series of
code because they come in useful when
creating a multi-connection with both clients
and servers. To get the most out of each of
these, save the server's connection as
multiconn-server.py and the client's code as
multiconn-client.py. When using both of them
to create a connection, simply run both and the
server will pick of the rest of the necessary
information.

Conclusion

Sockets are defined as programming commands that connect to networked systems. These could be the internet or local servers connected via a router or modem. They are important to receive information within the Python software. These connections can mean the difference between a quick processing speed and a function that can barely get off the floor.

Echo client and server processes and multi-connection processes are vital ways to get started in the programming game. Since it is often essential to have connection with an outside server (like the internet), it is one of the most useful tools within Python. Python contains libraries that are specifically tailored to help out with processing these transactions, and connecting your device to a server to run your business opens the gates to also including online transactions, partnerships with other online companies, and more.

Final Conclusion

You made it to the end of the book! Congratulations! Now that you have made the big move to start thinking about your future, take a moment to remember how far you have come. In the beginning, you may have known some things about Python, or you may have been a complete newbie to programming.

Now that your skills have advanced, it becomes even more necessary to start thinking of opportunities to grow your career. The job market is growing tremendously, and there is a market for successful coders. While machine intelligence is becoming more prominent online, there is always a market for those who can make changes and problem solve. Keep this in mind when you are worried about starting your career.

Where do you plan to go with the knowledge you have obtained from this book? If you are interested in the basics of Python and its advances, go over the basics in this book over and over, until it really starts to make sense. If you are interested in helping a company grow their emailing service, use our chapter to understand the basics, and use the code to jumpstart your way into your new career. If you want to become a stellar creator, we can tell you that there is always a market for people with those skills. With the games in this book, you should be able to create your own in no time. There are thousands, if not millions, of companies offering high-paying jobs to get the most out of their software, and you are well on your way to becoming one of those top competitors.

We have given you the basics of coding within Python, a programming language that is universally accepted as one of the most simple coding languages to learn. We have provided code and instruction to get you through some of the most difficult parts of Python. We have set up a basis for many different kinds of coding, including those that interact with the internet and a really fun game you can use to impress your friends. We promised that we could show you what being a coder is like, and the information in this book creates the perfect start to your coding journey.

We have covered the basics that you will need to start a career in programming, but there are many other subjects within this book that are essential to building a strong foundation.

Python is known for its versatility, so it is important to know a little about other applications you can use with Python. Fortunately, Python has a basis in internet and local operations, which means anyone can learn how to code and can do it from any location.

Learning to code it Python is like creating a world within another. Our own reality may become boring at times and offer little creative reprieve. However, Python keeps problem solving one of the most vital parts of creating code. After all, who does not like a challenge? Humans are known for their desire to make a difference in their lives, so why not you? It is time to use coding as your escape from harsh reality.

OOP is a great way to start thinking about code. Learning this subject is the first key to learning how databases and coding languages work. Through modules that help create real-time changes to code, you can create functions that will be saved within Python's library, available any time you need them. Though you might have never thought it possible, SMTP allows mail processing through Python. The code is already installed on Python's library, but adding additional libraries to help you with the heavy lifting is half the battle.

Likewise, SQL is an example of a database that creates tables and provides places to put useful information. Through the insert, update, select, and delete commands, you can create a software that easily distributed. SQL also offers the ability to share its tables with others connected to a server. Companies who look for coders want them to create software that is easy to use and makes their lives better. Spending time creating a database that looks as good as it works will get you that job.

Concurrent and parallel programming are the two main ways to process information in Python. They each have their good and bad points, but concurrent programming is the most common ways to set up a database. However, there are pitfalls to working with concurrent programming: deadlocks and race conditions tend to get in the way of an otherwise soothe process. Mutual exclusions and locks are the keys to keeping your programming running smoothly.

Finally, sockets are some of the most important parts of programming in Python. They offer connections to other hosts through networking. If you want to become one of the most sought-after coders, consider spending some time learning the intricacies of Python.

Expect the most out of yourself by pushing yourself to reach new boundaries. Make goals within Python to get the most experience out of it that you can. Python is available for everyone, but it can also be very specialized. In fact, once you have started your Python journey, no one will have the same code as you, and no one will have the same experiences you have. There are multiple ways to pick up new skills, and Python has the unique ability to handle most every subject.

The most important thing to take away from this book is its ability to change your career into something to which you have always aspired. Programming is not for the faint of heart, but it is for everyone who wants to delve into coding. Always remember, the future is always ready for you if you are willing to take it by the reins!

References

Anderson, J. (2019, March 25). An Intro to Threading in Python. Retrieved November 15, 2019, from https://realpython.com/intro-to-python-threading/.

Conditions. (n.d.). Retrieved November 13, 2019, from https://techwithtim.net/tutorials/python-programming/beginner-python-tutorials/conditions/.

de Langen, J. (2018, December 5). Sending Emails With Python. Retrieved November 14, 2019, from https://realpython.com/python-send-email/.

Duff, W. (2019, October 11). What Is an SMTP Server? Retrieved November 14, 2019, from https://sendgrid.com/blog/what-is-an-smtp-server/.

Encapsulation. (n.d.). Retrieved November 13, 2019, from https://pythonprogramminglanguage.com/encapsulation/.

Get Your Mac Ready for Python Programming. (2013, March 13). Retrieved November 11,

2019, from http://www.pyladies.com/blog/Get-Your-Mac-Ready-for-Python-Programming/.

Google. (n.d.). Python Quickstart | Gmail API | Google Developers. Retrieved November 13, 2019, from https://developers.google.com/gmail/api/quickstart/python.

Groff, J. R., & Weinberg, P. N. (2002). Sql: the complete reference (2nd ed.). New York, NY: McGraw-Hill Education - Europe.

Heba, K. T. (2019, September 24). Best Way to Learn Python (Step-by-Step Guide). Retrieved November 12, 2019, from https://www.afternerd.com/blog/learn-python/.

Installation. (n.d.). Retrieved November 14, 2019, from https://www.scipy.org/install.html.

Installation guide. (n.d.). Retrieved November 13, 2019, from http://doc.scrapy.org/en/latest/intro/install.html.

Jennings, N. (2018, August 17). Socket Programming in Python (Guide). Retrieved November 15, 2019, from https://realpython.com/python-sockets/#multi-connection-client-and-server.

Klein, B. (n.d.). Python Course. Retrieved November 13, 2019, from https://www.python-course.eu/python3_inheritance.php.

Kumar, N. (2019, August 28). Multithreading in Python: Set 2 (Synchronization). Retrieved November 15, 2019, from https://www.geeksforgeeks.org/multithreading-in-python-set-2-synchronization/.

Larson, Q. (2019, July 26). We asked 15,000 people who they are, and how they're learning to code. Retrieved November 7, 2019, from https://www.freecodecamp.org/news/we-asked-15-000-people-who-they-are-and-how-theyre-learning-to-code-4104e29b2781/.

Mindfire Solutions. (2017, April 24). Advantages and Disadvantages of Python Programming Language. Retrieved November 11, 2019, from https://medium.com/@mindfiresolutions.usa/advantages-and-disadvantages-of-python-programming-language-fd0b394f2121.

OverIQ. (n.d.). Inheritance and Polymorphism in Python. Retrieved November 13, 2019, from https://overiq.com/python-101/inheritance-and-polymorphism-in-python/.

PyCharm: the Python IDE for Professional Developers by JetBrains. (n.d.). Retrieved November 11, 2019, from https://www.jetbrains.com/pycharm/.

Python. (n.d.). re - Regular expression operations. Retrieved from https://docs.python.org/3/library/re.html.

Python. (n.d.). Web Frameworks for Python. Retrieved November 14, 2019, from https://wiki.python.org/moin/WebFrameworks/.

Python. (n.d.). 8.9. mutex - Mutual exclusion support. Retrieved November 15, 2019, from https://docs.python.org/2/library/mutex.html.

Python - Numbers. (n.d.). Retrieved November 12, 2019, from https://www.tutorialspoint.com/python/python_numbers.htm.

Python for Beginners. (n.d.). How to use Pillow, a fork of PIL. Retrieved November 14, 2019, from https://www.pythonforbeginners.com/gui/how-to-use-pillow.

Python for Beginners. (n.d.). Reading and Writing Files in Python. Retrieved November 13, 2019, from https://www.pythonforbeginners.com/files/reading-and-writing-files-in-python.

Python Programming. (n.d.). Converting PyGame to an Executable. Retrieved November 14, 2019, from https://pythonprogramming.net/converting-pygame-executable-cx_freeze/.

Real Python. (2019, March 16). Object-Oriented Programming (OOP) in Python 3. Retrieved November 13, 2019, from https://realpython.com/python3-object-oriented-programming/#what-is-object-oriented-programming-oop.

Ronquillo, A. (2019, January 23). Python's Requests Library (Guide). Retrieved November 13, 2019, from https://realpython.com/python-requests/.

Sturtz, J. (2018, October 26). Python Modules and Packages – An Introduction. Retrieved November 14, 2019, from https://realpython.com/python-modules-packages/#executing-a-module-as-a-script.

TurboSMTP. (n.d.). What is an SMTP port. Retrieved November 14, 2019, from https://serversmtp.com/port-for-smtp/.

Variables & Data Types. (n.d.). Retrieved November 12, 2019, from https://techwithtim.net/.

Vishal. (2019, September 9). Python MySQL Delete table Data [Complete Guide]. Retrieved November 15, 2019, from https://pynative.com/python-mysql-delete-data/.

What is Linux? (n.d.). Retrieved November 11, 2019, from https://www.linux.com/what-is-linux/